THE UNREASONABLE GUIDE

I WANT
YOU TO
CHEAT!

TO SERVICE AND QUALITY
IN ORGANISATIONS

Vanguard Education Ltd
Villiers House, 1 Nelson Street
Buckingham, MK18 1BU
www.lean-service.com

Published 1992
Re-printed 2002

Sub-edited by Jacky Woodwards

Printed and bound by Ecoutéz, Hemel Hempstead

ISBN 0 9519731 0 X

A director of customer services was accused
of cheating by his fellow board members.

He had conducted a satisfaction survey and
instructed his managers to visit every
customer who had rated the service less than
seven out of ten, and take whatever action
was necessary. The board took the view that
this was 'cheating' - after all, anyone could
improve their service ratings in this way!

The director would tell his managers this
story and implore them:

'I WANT YOU TO CHEAT!'

He didn't want them to behave immorally,
but he did want to free them of attitudes
that would impede improvement. His
fellow board members' ideas of fairness
might have been reasonable at some time in
the past, (although I have no idea when) but
pursuit of service quality, or any change for
that matter, sometimes requires an
unreasonable attitude.

Preface

It is ten years since we first published "I Want You To Cheat". Back then publishers told us it would not sell. It has sold 20,000 copies.

Since the book was first published we have learned a lot more about organisations, how work works and how to improve it. There was a temptation to re-write the book. However, I have resisted the temptation because this little book works – it is a good introduction to a better way of thinking about the design and management of work.

I hope you will agree.

John Seddon

March 2002

For
Flora, Jodie and Angela

Contents

About this book

There has been much enthusiastic talk about service and quality in organisations. To date, three general approaches have appeared in the marketplace: quality education, customer-first initiatives and establishing procedures (for example BS5750, a quality standard). The advocates of each promise a new tomorrow. None delivers its promise consistently.

There is, however a consensus that improvement in service and quality requires a change in culture. This means getting people to think and behave differently.

Many organisations have embarked on programmes of change but remained oblivious to that fact that the very thing they have to change – their culture – has undermined their efforts. For example, having watched a well-known financial services organisation present the results of their service and quality initiative, it seemed to me that the essential message was that they had been doing it for seven years, had spent more than ten million pounds, yet they were still no better than their competitors! Investment of this size in anything else would be scrutinised much more carefully.

People are coming to realise that service and quality cannot be achieved by superficial means. On the contrary, to achieve real quality often requires a fundamental reappraisal of the way the organisation works. Roles must be redesigned, procedures reviewed, new systems built and so on. Change will only occur if left to unreasonable people, for they are the ones who will change things rather than put up with that which is clearly wrong.

People need to think, 'Why do I do this?' or 'How could we do this differently or better?' People need to be unreasonable. They need to question the assumptions that govern today's practice and redesign the way they work in the light of what the organisation is setting out to achieve. It is not just the leader's job to think unreasonably, people involved in work at all levels will have good ideas about how to improve the work they do. The purpose of this book is to encourage unreasonable thinking.

It is not intended that this should be a comprehensive guide to the issues of organisational change. Much use will be made of observations and stories as these are more memorable than theoretical text. More importantly, they provide illustrations of many key principles which need to be understood when improving the performance of organisations. The hope is that people in organisations will be spurred into thumping the table and stop putting up with those things that clearly need to change. If they do, I hope that they are fortunate enough to have good managers.

Chapter 1

Believing in Customers

Trust customers

> *While on holiday in Florida, I met a man who ran a small chain of restaurants in Toronto, Canada. They were fast food restaurants with an average meal price of $12 per head. He told me that over the last couple of years he'd been doing a lot to improve service and quality. One of the boldest ideas had been to put up a sign in his restaurants saying 'If it's not to your satisfaction it's on the house!' Of course his friends thought he was crazy and the reader might think him crazy too. They claimed that the place would be full of freeloaders and soon he would be out of business.*

Well that didn't happen and, if you think about it, it is unlikely that it would. If customers *were* cheats they would soon become known to the restaurant manager. Only the most brazen would take up the challenge to go repeatedly to the same restaurant and demand free food.

What was the result? Customer complaints stayed at the same level but the cost of dealing with complaints went down and turnover went up. The signs not only sent a clear message to customers but also, and equally importantly, they sent a clear message to the staff. (Of course to behave this way you also have to have some confidence in the quality of your goods!)

> *You may have heard the story of a customer who repeatedly complained about his delivered pizzas and consequently kept getting them free of charge. The exasperated restaurant manager invited him to come and show them how he'd like his pizza made (and paid his taxi fare). Even following this the customer continued to complain. The manager had reached the position where he was prepared to refuse his custom but instead gave the customer free pizza for life. He thought that the word of mouth advertising would be worth the trivial investment.*

What each of these organisations did was trust their customers – absolutely and unequivocally. They didn't take the view that customers were going to take advantage of them if they possibly could. Their attitude was that they were running a service business and therefore, whatever else the customer got, they were going to get exemplary service (or else they would get free goods).

Compare these examples with the recent spate of 'service guarantees' in the UK. For example, utility companies are promising refunds if they fail to meet their service standard. At one level these promises look the same – the customer gains if the standard is not maintained. In reality, they have quite a different effect.

Organisations are building bureaucracies of standards-setting committees and service guarantee claims departments. This work adds to their costs and has the underlying assumption that they will always fail to perform to 100 per cent and will always have to administer (whether defensively or not) claims made against them. The whole of this effort provides the wrong focus. Everybody involved is spending time on what's not working instead of working on how to improve things.

Furthermore, other staff begin to use the 'guarantees' as ways of helping problems to go away. It becomes easier to give customers a number to ring for the claim form rather than attend to the customer's needs. The irony of service guarantees is that they can begin to spoil the relationship ('Win ten pounds – catch us doing something wrong!'). Imagine how you would feel if you were told you could claim half off your next car rental when you have just missed a charter flight and have a tired and emotional family on your hands because the rental car broke down! In addition, how many customers would be keen on the idea of having to fill in a claim form to get any justice? What does the customer want? The customer wants to be dealt with by someone who can solve his problem and make reparations where appropriate.

Who are the people who are most likely to be able to judge what should be done for a customer when something has gone wrong? The people in the front line. I believe the rise in service guarantees reflects a serious problem: the failure of management to trust people in the front line.

Trust staff

The best service organisations have people in the front line capable of taking immediate responsibility to resolve customer problems. To run an organisation in this way means having staff who know what to do. While we would usually look for such guidance in job descriptions and customer service policy manuals, the approach I like best is one sentence long:

'Use your own best judgement'

> *This, a friend of mine tells me, is the customer service policy of a US department store. Introducing this policy takes one hour of the induction training programme. Why does it take one hour? Well apparently some people don't understand what 'use your own best judgement' means. The assumption here is that the people in the front line are usually in the best position to determine how to solve a customer's problem. They are the ones most familiar with what has been going on and therefore know what action seems fair or appropriate.*

Most people understand the logic of this but some of them would say, 'But what if I really feel I can't decide?' This organisation thinks that the answer is to ask the customer. They know that research shows that customers would normally spend less of the organisation's money than the organisation does in resolving a problem. Most customers only want an apology and acknowledgement of their complaint. Employees then ask what should they do if the customer can't decide. 'Well then,' says the organisation, 'ask one of your colleagues and between the three of you see if you can sort something out'. It is only when all these approaches have failed that staff are advised to consult a manager.

How often in our organisations do we insist that people don't do *anything* without going through at least one or more levels of management?

The extraordinary thing is that managers can rarely add any value to solving problems. After all they are further away

from what's happening. There is also an additional problem
in that if the manager appears on the scene and does solve the
problem the customer will not bother to talk to the staff the
next time – he will just demand to see the manager. We spoil
not only customer relationships with staff, but also staff
relationships with management.

Service is the creation of value

The relationship with the customer is everything. If it is
right, you are assured continued business, loyalty and word of
mouth advertising. For service is the creation of value – that's
all it is. It's about the customer's emotional experience of the
organisation, the customer's perception. The word
'perception' is used deliberately. It is not enough to deliver
good service. The *customer* must *perceive* that it is good
service.

Think of any organisation you regularly deal with. How
do employees treat customers with special needs or
problems? As an annoyance or as an opportunity? How often
do you have to run the 'organisational maze' from one
department to another to get your needs met?

Service is delivered by the system – not just the people in the front line

It's not a matter of the 'customer friendliness' of the
person dealing with you. It's more a matter of how the whole
system in which he or she works supports or hinders their
dealings with you.

> *Have you ever stayed at home for a 'fridge or washing
> machine service engineer? Sometimes all goes well, he
> arrives on time, has the part and completes the work. All*

*too often though, problems occur with timing, parts and,
most importantly, the ability to make a definite
commitment as to when the work will be completed.*

*When things don't go well engineers are often unable to
tell you when they'll get a part. They may have been
routed in such a way as to make it difficult for them to
make all their calls, and the forms they carry would
appear to have been designed by someone who had
deliberately set out to make 'getting things' difficult.*

Good service engineers are supported by people who see it
as *their* job to continually improve the *support* they offer the
engineer, in other words they try to make it easy for the
engineers to serve the customer. They think about their work
in this way because they are following the example of their
managers. But too few managers have given up the belief that
engineers are difficult people from whom it is their task to
extract the most. They view the system of stores, despatch and
other support functions as a means of controlling engineers
rather than a means of enabling them to perform effectively.

Of course managers can't solve the problems by handing
over their powers tomorrow, but they can start talking about
the things that matter – the things that stop service personnel
from doing what they're paid for.

A key issue for service design, therefore, is how to ensure
that people in the front line feel equipped to make
commitments to customers. In turn, you have to ensure that
others in the organisation see their role as helping these
people to honour the commitments they make. Front-line
people need to know who to contact when they have a
problem and they need direct access to them (going through
the boss can only slow things down and may make matters
worse). For those contacted it means treating the front-line
person as *their* customer.

The issue here is attitude, not procedures or education, although they may help. Attitudes in organisations have been too heavily influenced by notions of hierarchy, functionalism and control. People responsible for organisation design think more about things they can measure than what's happening to the customer.

> *A director of quality was shopping in his supermarket one Saturday afternoon. He was packing his goods at the checkout and, being a rather fastidious individual, he was trying to ensure that his iced goods went in one box, his fresh food in another, tins in another and so on. Unfortunately he couldn't work as fast as the boy operating the point-of-sale terminal. The speed with which the boy could pass things over the light was such that he soon found himself in difficulty. He asked the boy to stop. The boy refused and continued to pass items over the light The director, surprised and a little disgruntled, did his best to pack his boxes. The boy finished ringing up his goods and at that point turned to help. 'How extraordinary,' the director remarked, 'when I asked you to stop and help me just now you didn't, you insisted on carrying on'. 'Well', said the young man, 'when this machine is turned on it is counting how quickly I pass things over the light.'*

Compare this with another supermarket where every Saturday extra staff are employed in the checkout area to help people like the director. The manager is not allowed to redeploy them. The customer's experience of the organisation is paramount to the business.

While productivity of a checkout operator in a supermarket is important, measuring it at the point-of-sale can be counter-productive. What counts at the supermarket checkout is the customer's experience, which is governed only in part by the speed of processing goods. Management, believing that this measure will help them to control

performance, may actually be undermining what really
matters – customer care!

Service means attending to the basics

Taking a car for a service is an experience that most
people are familiar with and one which, generally speaking,
falls into two categories. One is typified by a receptionist
who greets the customer by name and who knows why he is
there. He or she attends well to the customer's needs. In the
other category one often finds the reception is too busy or the
receptionist is answering the telephone. The customer is not
well attended to, rather he is treated as a necessary evil.

> *While exploring these differences with a group of
> managers, a man who had recently become the owner of
> a Volvo said that he was astounded by the quality of
> service he was receiving at his local Volvo garage. When
> invited to describe the service he said that he was dealt
> with by name not by job title. The garage asked when he
> wanted the car taken in, rather than telling him when
> they could fit it in, they wanted to know when he wanted
> it back, where he would be going that day and whether
> he needed any help with alternative transport. They also
> asked whether there were any special things he wanted
> them to pay attention to. 'I was flabbergasted'. he said.*

Furthermore, when he arrived he was greeted by name.
Apparently it was normal procedure to check the number-
plates of new customers and find their name on the
worksheet. If you review the above list of what flabbergasted
that manager, you'll find it is basically how we would all like
to be treated. The issue is not having the idea but organising
to make it happen. So often service comes down to doing the
basic well. The first requirement is to seek customer
perceptions with a willingness to do something about them.

Listening to customers is the key

Listening to customers should govern the way an organisation works if it is serious about service and quality. Initiatives by companies in measuring satisfaction must be welcomed, but on the whole people are still fearful of listening to their customers. When managers are asked why they do not survey their customers their answers show that they do not regard this as a priority issue or even believe that it is important: 'We know our customers'; 'We did a survey last year'; 'We keep an eye on complaints'. Yet it is surprising how much time customers are prepared to give to the endeavour if asked (and I do not mean asking in the manner of the retreating waiter who, having enquired if everything is alright, is expecting an affirmative reply). There seems to be a fear of going out and listening to customers. Perhaps people are fearful that the customer might want things changed and that meeting these demands would entail too much disruption.

Despite the advantages of face-to-face contact, many organisations pursue research into customer satisfaction as something that they must keep at a distance (perhaps in the best tradition of research). Recently I met an organisation who wanted to create such sensitive customer measures that they would be able to predict when a customer was likely to change allegiance. Researchers were employed to gather a variety of data to be developed into models. I was reminded of my experience as a prison psychologist, learning of the application of catastrophic theory to predicting prison riots.

> *Able psychologists employed in central offices were working to model the social psychology of prison behaviour. They took a series of behavioural measures and plotted them on the mathematical (catastrophe) model. The research was being conducted over an extended period and psychologists like myself were*

made aware of the purposes and methods through periodic seminars.

One day a riot occurred. The data did not predict it. Quite naturally the inclination of the scientists was to treat it as an opportunity to refine the model and therefore they set about weighting or altering variables. It occurred to others that if you wanted to know the likelihood of a prison riot occurring, it would be best to ask the officers who man the wings – they, after all, live in the community and have a very clear idea of what is happening.

The same rule applies to customers. People who deal with the customers every day have a good idea of what upsets them and which ones are so dissatisfied they are likely to withdraw their custom. The trouble is we tend not to ask them.

Use customer data to drive change

And why don't we? Why do we spend thousands of pounds of marketplace research that is, on the whole, unattainable instead of listening to and acting on what our customers tell us? Perhaps it is because senior managers – the decision-makers – have been seduced into believing they can run the business more like a spectator of the sport than an involved player. If that's a little strong perhaps it's that we don't know how to question what we do, we don't know how to be unreasonable.

A British bank pursued an unusual variant of customer research – 'mystery shoppers'. Eventually the union complained because staff disliked the idea of being spied on by consultants who would pose as customers and write reports of their experiences.

> *A Canadian bank pursued the same notion but used real customers. A large group of customers was invited to a meeting where the scheme was explained and they were invited to participate. They all did. The customers were asked to write to the local branch manager of their experiences every time they used the bank. The results were fascinating. The bank found that different branches had different types of customers – people with varying service and product needs. As a consequence of this survey branches were able to organise themselves more particularly for their customers.*

It is an astonishing story (for bankers). Bankers have always implicitly equated service with standards and standardisation – you can rely on it being the same in all branches. The Canadian bank is, to my knowledge, the first differentiated bank in the world!

When bankers hear this story at conferences they want to know immediately the name of the bank. This is understandable but the wrong question to ask. The question ought to be: 'What is to stop us doing something as common-sense and straightforward as that?'. (Answer: your culture!)

Listening to customers ought to be the starting point of a service of quality programme. Whatever you learn should govern the way the organisation works. It is extraordinary how many organisations proclaim their commitment to the customer and yet do little to gather any useful information. In my experience, organisations that do listen to customers ('What do we need to do for you to give us a rating of ten?') move quickly. One moved from the bottom to the top of an independent customer survey (not the one they were using themselves, but a useful benchmark) in only one year. What they had in their favour was the right attitude – listen and act.

An extraordinary example of service responsiveness was provided by a recent television documentary on banks. The story was a comparison of how two car dealerships (one American, one British) had been treated by their banks when they ran into similar problems: one had an accountant who made a big mistake, the other an accountant who ran off with lots of money. As a matter of interest the US organisation suffered the greatest loss.

When the British dealer went to his bank he was asked to hire a firm of expensive consultants to prepare a plan. This he did, finding that their plan agreed with his own recommendations. The bank accepted the plan but failed to communicate with its sister organisation (a merchant bank) which held the customer's loan. The merchant bank called in the receivers. After a fortnight's wrangling the receivers were removed but the customer had to pay their bill. The customer not only had to put up a fight to stay in business, but he also had to bear all of the costs.

By contrast, the American dealer was met with understanding and concern. After a ten-minute conversation he left his bank knowing that together they would find a way out of his present situation and prevent it from ever happening again. He faced no additional costs and gained considerable peace of mind.

The circumstances leading to such different responses show that each bank had an entirely different way of thinking about how they conducted their business. For banks, as well as many other organisations, it is the whole system that needs to change if real advances in service and quality are to be made. For this to happen, people need to change the way in which they think. The change is unlikely to occur while thinking is influenced by notions of hierarchy.

The unreasonable guide – believing in customers

- Trust customers.

- Trust staff.

- Service is the creation of value.

- Service is delivered by the system – not just the people in the front line.

- Service means attending to the basics.

- Listening to customers is the key.

- Use customer data to drive change.

Chapter 2

Sins of Hierarchy

Associating hierarchical status with importance

Managers often operate under the mistaken assumption that their hierarchical status is a reflection of their importance within the organisation.

> *The head office management of an organisation had embarked on a programme they called Visible Management. This entailed spending some time doing a front-line job. They were supposed to be using the opportunity to remind themselves about conditions in that part of the organisation where the money is made. Instead they explained to staff the difficulties experienced in head office and gave the impression that the work head office had to do would be made much easier if the field staff would 'do as they should!'*

There are times, for example during an uncertain economic climate, when an organisation may want to examine the role of its management more closely.

> A British retail organisation shed 900 people without affecting the ratio of customer service personnel to customers. They took 600 people from the stores and 300 from head office. Those working in the stores were heads of departments who spent most of their time compiling reports for the 300 in head office. The organisation took the view that they would probably do just as well in serving customers without these people. That is the issue for middle-management: are they adding value to the service?

The assumptions that only those who have attained hierarchical status have valid opinions can lead to valuable opportunities to improve service being lost.

> In the shop of a leading fashion retailer a customer asked what would be coming in for the new season. The assistant didn't know. She explained that the decisions were made by head office and that she would only find out herself when it was sent. The organisation had a very efficient point-of-sale information system. They could track what was being sold and change what they distributed accordingly. All excellent objectives but they missed the opportunity to discuss the next season's stock with their customers. As a result, important information (what the customers would like) was ignored and the front line became isolated and less capable of dealing with customers.

In situations like this, head office becomes more like 'big brother', and 'big brother' demands reports.

Using reports as substitutes for action

Consider how much management time in organisations is given over to the production of monthly reports. In one organisation each branch consumed six man-days writing their report. These were six man-days that could have been used productively in the business. This view was put to the operations director. 'Oh no', he said 'you don't understand. Monthly reports are very important. They tell me what's going on in the business.' Wrong. Monthly reports were telling him what people *wanted* to tell him about what was going on in the business.

People are not inclined to pass on bad news in their monthly reports, Mistakes or failures get hidden: people at the top are not in full possession of the facts. Consequently they risk making decisions on inadequate information. It is likely that less learning and improvement will take place in this situation and problems will certainly be created if senior managers act without a good knowledge of the current state of business.

If you really want to know what's going on, you have to talk to the people who do the work. More importantly, they should feel free to talk to each other. Hierarchical thinking encourages everybody to 'look up' all the time rather than out to the customer. When an organisation sets out to improve service and quality, the attention of the people who need to be engaged in the problem is diverted upwards.

> *A maintenance organisation was obliged to report the number of average breakdowns per month to its European HQ. For years it had done so by taking branch averages, averaging those out to produce regional averages and then doing the same again to produce the UK figure. In the course of a programme of change it was pointed out to them that an average of an average is a*

meaningless number (ask a statistician to explain this to you if you need to). As they were already committed to drop reports which were consuming management's time, this was an easy choice to make – but they kept sending a number into headquarters for a while. After all, they didn't want to be the first to stop presenting expected reports, and in any case it would do no harm as they'd been sending meaningless information for years!

One February, in the course of an organisation analysis, I found myself sitting with a finance director. Among other things, he told me that they had a significant problem with monies owed to them by customers who had yet to be billed. In fact there was £1.2 million in cash which should have been collected from customers but was still outstanding because billing had not proceeded. He said that he had first become aware of the problem in November and that he had assigned a subordinate, Mark, to the task of investigating it. When I asked what progress had been made he admitted that he did not yet know. I left the interview with the extraordinary feeling that if the sum involved was £1.2 last November, and in February he still didn't know what was happening, there might be something worth finding out.

The following day I called Mark. He told me that the problem lay in the procedures between operations and sales. When I asked when he had become aware of this he replied that the nature of the problem had been understood by early December. I enquired as to what he was expected to do about it and was given the answer that when he had time he was going to write a report for submission to his boss.

Three whole months had gone by since the problem was first identified. There were people in the organisation who understood the problem, but the unwritten rule was that no action could be taken until a report had been submitted.

If you owned a large country estate and wanted a croquet lawn you would probably instruct your estate manager. He, in turn, would tell the head gardener, the head gardener would tell the lawn superintendent, and the lawn superintendent would, in turn, instruct the boy. If you wanted to know how your croquet lawn was progressing, what would you do? In all probability you would take a look the next time you were passing that way. Why don't we do this in organisations? In a typical organisation we would ask the hierarchy how things were going and, of course, we would hear only what they thought we wanted to hear.

Believing that communication through the hierarchy works

> In a review of the efficacy of briefing groups in organisations, a journalist uncovered a number of problems:
>
> 1. The information was constantly changing.
>
> 2. The recipients of the information often failed to see its relevance.
>
> 3. The managers responsible for disseminating it did so with different levels of enthusiasm.
>
> In the interests of balance, the journalist invited a consultant experienced in briefing groups to comment. Essentially the consultant's view was that the organisations weren't carrying out their briefings well enough and that they should try harder. He didn't seem inclined to explore why.

Organisations mould the way people behave, sometimes deliberately and sometimes through neglect. Either way, organisations give people expectations about how to behave and encourage or discourage them accordingly. A central plank in organisational thinking is hierarchy – it governs how we think about jobs and how people should behave towards one another.

Thinking of management's job as control

Traditionally, managers see their role as one of optimising their resources. Work is organised on a functional basis; the argument being that this makes it easier to control because one can measure the results achieved and resources used. Performance goals are cascaded down the organisation. As the goals get nearer to that part of the organisation where the work is actually done, they become imposed numerical goals with the associated measures for control. While the thinking is rational, the effect on the organisation is often devastating. Each department sees its purpose as the achievement of short-term measurable goals. Often departments come into conflict and some will strive to meet their own goals regardless of the effect on other departments or the organisation as a whole.

Management by control encourages people to look inwards at their own structures rather than outwards to the customer. People feel that accomplishment comes from meeting the controls rather than meeting customer needs. Management by control becomes a self-reinforcing phenomenon leading to complacency; people assume that everything is going well if they meet the controls. By the time the organisation realises that it is off course, it's usually too late.

Notions of hierarchy and service are basically incompatible. Hierarchy encourages people to the view that they are there to serve the boss. In service organisations we should be encouraging people to the view that they are there to serve the customer.

The re-education of management begins with the destruction of hierarchical *thinking*. It is true that organisations are reducing levels of management to good effect, but this does not mean that people have changed their way of thinking.

On 'customer-service' seminars, managers are encouraged to think of their organisation as an upside-down triangle. Instead of being a hierarchy (like a pyramid), it is shown to be supporting all those people who spend their time with customers. They see the logic of this and say that it's a good idea, but too few realise just what action must be taken and which practices must be abolished. At the very least it means that managers must not demand that their staff are always doing things for *them*, after all the staff are there to serve the customer. Even worse, people often feel that their job is simply to do as they are told, the implications being not to use initiative, break procedures or do anything they shouldn't.

In the days of craft guilds people were respected for what they could do and had pride in their accomplishments. Doing only as you are told can have a devastating impact on pride and, therefore, commitment.

> An administration clerk sent a customer five acknowledgements, each as a separate letter in the same post. The letters had been generated automatically by the system. Normally, she would have taken the time to rewrite the five because her work was to get the daily numbers out. She was serving her boss, not the customer.

Misusing numbers

So often it is the use of numbers that encourages hierarchical thinking. It is ironic that thinking hierarchically often creates *abuse* of numbers.

If you ran an hotel you would be concerned, quite rightly, with numbers that tell you about performance. You would collect, for example, numbers on customer satisfaction, bedroom occupancy, revenue and costs in various departments, and so on.

What often happens in hotel chains is that numbers in individual hotels are added up to become the numbers for the area manager. These numbers are, in turn, added up again to become the numbers for the regional manager. The regional managers' numbers are then added up and these become the numbers for the operations director.

There are two problems here. Firstly, once the numbers are added up they have less meaning and therefore are less useful. Secondly, and more importantly, aggregated numbers encourage managers to send instructions without understanding why. For example, a manager two levels up the chain would send a missive for the hotels to reduce the costs of a line item (for example laundry costs) without understanding the impact of the instruction on the hotels.

It is at the operating unit level that the business takes place. Numbers produced at this level can be used meaningfully to make decisions about the business. It is relevant to use comparative information (for example between hotels or between time periods) to consider what is being achieved or consumed by operating units in providing service to their customers. Numbers of this sort will encourage attention to process (see Chapter 6) especially if they are given to the people who do the work. When they are added up, however, they lose their meaning and become tools with which managers attempt to exert control. It is a fact that, more often than not, the result is that the business becomes more out of control.

Aggregating numbers, making reports and serving the boss all reinforce the notion that the boss knows best. This view is part of a wider traditional philosophy – namely that it is the responsibility of the boss to set standards and control performance.

Believing that management decides and staff work

The customers in a supermarket queue were beginning to voice their frustration. There was only one checkout open and the queue was long. Two members of staff were in the queue too, waiting to pay for snacks they had bought for their break! As soon as people began voicing their frustrations, the two staff members moved aside to allow others ahead in the queue. The customers suggested they should man their workstations and the staff agreed but explained that their manager insisted that they take breaks at specified times. No-one saw the sense of the manager's behaviour; the staff even asked the customers to talk to him. This was clearly one of many frustrations for the staff.

Who is in the best position to make sensible decisions?

A family arrived at a 'pub chain' restaurant one evening at 6.45. They had missed the 6.30 half-price special and were told to wait for a table at 7.15. After waiting a while, two members of the family walked through the restaurant to use the toilets. They noticed empty tables.

It transpired, from talking to the staff, that management had determined that a section of the restaurant would be kept closed during the early period. At 7.15 extra staff would arrive and the whole restaurant would open. Presumably they had decided that this was the best way to keep costs down and thus make reasonable profits.

*It presented staff with a problem. Quite often they had to
deal with customers who couldn't appreciate why they
had to wait when tables were obviously ready.*

*When asked if the managers ever spent time with the
waitresses to find out about how they worked and what
the customers needed, the staff said they rarely saw
them. Apparently the managers spent their time in some
'ivory tower' remote from the heart of the business.*

*Clearly, the staff didn't think much of their managers, but
it was more than their jobs were worth to challenge a
management decision.*

There is no choice about addressing the sins of hierarchy
if you are serious about service and quality. Everything and
anything may need to change; structure, information, job
design, relationships between functions and so on. With
change will come an increase in problems, and as these are
identified people will look to their managers to solve them. If
managers operate from a hierarchical perspective, rushing out
to issue an instruction, apply a solution or perhaps leave a
procedure for future occurrences before they disappear again,
little change of substance is likely to be achieved.

Management have to realise that successful change starts
with helping the people who serve the customer to make
decisions about how to improve that service. The problem is
that too many managers believe their attention should be
given to output – a position from which they are unable to
make decisions about change.

Chapter 3

Attention to Output

The unreasonable guide – sins of hierarchy

- Associating hierarchical status with importance.

- Using reports as substitutes for action.

- Believing that communication through the hierarchy works.

- Thinking of management's job as control.

- Misusing numbers.

- Believing that management decides and staff work.

If you manage by attention to output, people cheat!

High-performance work teams are becoming more commonplace in manufacturing organisations. They are designed in accordance with the view that if you give people more responsibility for their work they become more productive. The teams take responsibility for inventory and have responsibility for measuring and recording their own output and quality.

With the development of such self-managing work teams, the role of the foreman has disappeared. As a consequence, the relationship between the team and its manager is significant in determining whether or not the concept actually succeeds. Broadly speaking we have found two types of manager in this situation. For the sake of the example we will call them Manager A and Manager B.

Manager A sits in an office somewhere off the production area and studies the daily or weekly production figures produced by the work teams. When a figure appears that (for some reason) he does not like, he emerges from his office to pay attention to the team on the machine in question. Under these conditions we find that work team members lie by falsifying their output or quality reports. Why do they do this? The reason is simple. The only way to keep that fool in his office is to feed him the wrong information! Nobody likes trouble, and by lying, the work team can manage to avoid it.

Manager B, on the other hand, spends a fair proportion of his time with the team doing the work. He expresses interest and concern about the quality of supplies coming to them, their machine operations and the management of inventory and associated problems. He also discusses with them what is being done to improve the quality of output. Under such conditions it is not necessary to lie, everybody knows what is going on.

The same phenomenon occurs in service organisations (in fact from a service or quality point of view there is no distinction between manufacturing and service organisations).

> A financial services company decided to embark on a quality improvement programme. As ever, the easiest things to count were the pieces of paper going through the system. People were required to fill in forms at the end of each working day to say, for example, how many items had been dealt with during the day, how many were still outstanding, how many were in progress and so on.
>
> In order to avoid management scrutiny directed at their unit, people would return unopened post to the post room and record 'no cases outstanding' on their work return. One consequence, of course, was that some post was counted twice. Not only was an improvement in productivity unlikely, but also the data were becoming less reliable.

People don't behave in this way because they want to be difficult; the reason is that they are being treated as part of the problem instead of part of the solution. People who do the work have good ideas about what quality means and can be helped with their ideas about how to measure and improve it. It is the managers' role to join with people in solving the problem of what measurement to use; they should also adopt an attitude of testing measurement rather than 'testing' people.

Management's job is attention to process, not function

Any service is made up of processes which cross organisational boundaries, so managers need to rid themselves of any hierarchical or territorial perspectives and be prepared to invest their time with the people whose work is performed across these boundaries. Manufacturers are now learning the same lessons. Although they have become more adept at quality measurement as it applies to what they make, they are recognising that the way people work together has an enormous impact on performance. And the way people work together is governed more by the way they are managed than by anything else.

Many managers have grown up in their organisations. Consequently they think they are familiar with how the work is done. After all, they themselves once did it. Unfortunately, many of them do not recognise just how much things have changed. Blind to their lack of knowledge they make decisions which they believe will improve things but which, in fact, may contribute to major disasters.

Making changes on inadequate information leads to costly mistakes

A maintenance organisation had grown rapidly by acquisition. Each of the acquired companies had its own procedures and practices. Clearly there was an opportunity to make efficiency gains by standardising procedures. On the advice of consultants, groups of managers were brought together to make decisions about the systems and procedures for the newly integrated organisation.

The group responsible for the spares system determined that it would be most efficient to organise nationally, using a system similar to that being operated by one of the original companies. The decision was announced and the new system implemented. Some unfortunate consequences followed. Managers in most of the merging companies had been held accountable for the cost of spares held locally. These figures were still being used to determine branch profitability and, therefore, the manager's bonus. Under the new system, where spares were treated as a national resource, one branch manager could, in an emergency, order a spare from another. As the cost of spares held locally effectively counted against a manager in his bonus scheme, it soon became common practice to hold minimal spares locally and order them as emergency items from nearby branches when required. The additional cost associated with transportation was the immediate wasteful consequence, but worse was to come.

*To avoid losing spares to nearby branches, managers began to stop logging some items on the national system. Quite rightly their concern was to maintain a level of service to **their** customers. The practice of hiding spares resulted in two problems. First, the unreliability of the national system, and second the increase in the cost of spares held throughout the organisation. In circumstances such as these, senior managers can only respond with drastic measures. In this case they stopped managers buying spares by reducing their authority levels. The first person to be affected was the customer.*

The team responsible for the new architecture had not considered its implication. If they had understood how the process already in place was working, they would have been able to determine what change was required from management. Furthermore, they would have been able to see the requirements for a change in the reward systems. Their single biggest failure was that they did not go to local managers with the new ideas and ask the question, 'How can we make this work?' When their system was implemented, the inevitable consequences followed.

Treat people as part of the solution, not part of the problem

It became apparent to the managers of a maintenance organisation that some engineers were not being as productive as they might be. When given a list of calls for the day only some engineers would complete them all.

Others would appear to be lost to the system. Some, for example, would report that they were being detained at jobs for longer than expected, and others would call service control towards the end of the day to return their unanswered calls to have them reassigned to other engineers.

The problem, management decided, was in the allocation of calls to engineers. Obviously, if engineers were given one call at a time and were told to call back to receive their next, then their activity would be under greater control and they would, therefore, be more productive. They had seen such a system working elsewhere. They decided to make this change and announced it on a Monday morning. While rumours had been rife the week before, the only information about what was to change was given by announcement at 8.30 at the start of the Monday morning shift. The managers then left the site.

Service control staff carried on as usual. They allocated a full day's work to those engineers who they knew could be trusted to complete their calls and work productively, but only one or two jobs at a time to those engineers with a reputation for laziness.

Of course the problem was not solved. Unproductive engineers were effectively being accommodated by service control staff. The managers who made decisions based on utilisation numbers were too remote from the work to understand who the unproductive engineers were or what could be done to improve their productivity. The irony of this story is that much of the information was available if only they had asked. The managers, however, viewed their task as getting what they could out of 'them' (the engineers and despatchers), rather than encouraging 'them' to take responsibility for improving their performance. The people were being treated as part of the problem rather than part of the solution, a perspective which encourages 'productivity' thinking (see Chapter 7).

The most sophisticated form of cheating we've found to date involved a customer satisfaction survey. The organisation had distributed surveys to customers through the sales force and had found that customers were being persuaded to give good ratings. In order to obtain more objective information, they announced to the sales force that the next survey would be sent without their knowledge to a cross-section of their customers.

Knowing that his salary would be affected by the result, a branch manager sent his own customer survey immediately to all his customers. He sorted his returns into 'happy' and 'unhappy' and then sent the unhappy customers a letter explaining that an administrative error might mean that they would receive another survey in the near future. If they did, they were asked to ignore it. What a wonderful application of ingenuity to problem solving: what a tragedy that his ingenuity was not more productively employed.

The unreasonable guide – attention to output

- If you manage by attention to output, people cheat!

- Management's job is attention to process, not function.

- Making changes on inadequate information leads to costly mistakes.

- Treat people as part of the solution, not part of the problem.

Chapter 4

Procedures and Quality

Procedures reflect attitude

A newly appointed customer services director arrived at his desk on a Friday morning. Before him he found a pile of papers. On enquiry as to what they were, he was told that they formed the accredited BS5750 escalation procedure, which simply meant the result of u procedure which produced a list of customers likely to call and complain in the following week. He asked where the papers had come from and was informed that they had been passed to him from the regional directors who had met the previous evening. The information was obtained by them from the district managers' Thursday morning meeting, and they, in turn, had received the figures from the Wednesday evening meeting held with the engineers.

The director's response was to cancel the whole procedure immediately and instruct his managers to take the information on dissatisfied customers directly from the engineers on Wednesday evening, contact the customers at once and make a definite commitment to solve their problems.

Two weeks later the chairman became upset. He was convinced that the switchboard had been told to stop putting complaining customers through to him. Clearly for him it was quite normal to receive a lot of customer complaints.

The view has been expressed that the 'procedures merchants' are taking over quality. There is undoubted merit in the philosophy underlying BS5750 / ISO 9000. (These are UK / international standards applying to quality management systems.) The problems do not lie in philosophy but in practice, and practice of course, is governed by attitude.

The problems start with the exclusion of any customer satisfaction measurement in the standard (it is merely recommended in advice notes rather than being part of the standard to be audited). Without this measurement where is the yardstick against which to consider procedures? The answer has to be some kind of internal focus, but if the people with an internal focus have the attitude that we should always do things the way we have done them in the past, then introducing the standard means institutionalising waste and possibly ensuring that service will never get better.

The operations director of a construction company compared the efficiencies of UK and US contractors. The US contractors were considerably ahead of their counterparts in the UK. He attributed most of the problems to filling in forms in order to comply with procedures. In the US he saw that more initiative and 'rule flexibility' was used to get the job done. This was in stark contrast to the British attitude, which could be summarised by the expression, 'Nothing moves in here without the right paperwork'.

Do procedures make it easy to serve customers?

The paradox for service organisations is that procedures must be flexible enough to cater for customer needs. The associated attitude is to think 'The way we do things here is governed by what our customers need.' Do you remember the Canadian bank in Chapter 1? They took the view that procedures in different branches should accommodate the different needs of the customers. In most banks, procedures are used to create standardisation – a sure way to alienate the customer.

When writing out a cheque for school fees, Roger realised that his personal account would be overdrawn by a relatively small amount. He wrote to the bank to explain the situation and to tell them that the overdraft would be repaid within a matter of weeks (he knew he had money coming). Roger travels frequently. On arriving home from one of his trips he found a letter from the bank acknowledging his letter and asking him to complete a form to establish an overdraft facility. Roger was busy, looked at the form, decided it was time-consuming and unnecessary and went back to work.

Next time he arrived home there was a second letter from the bank, telling him that his account was overdrawn (which he knew) and that if he didn't make the necessary arrangements they would be obliged to take further steps. Roger was not impressed, and neither did he have the energy to fill in the form. Away he went to work, returning only two days later to find a third letter threatening that any further cheques drawn on his account would be stopped and the bank would institute proceedings against him.

Roger wrote a letter of complaint to the most senior manager in the branch outlining the situation. The response from the bank manager was good. He cancelled the charges made on the account, and gave Roger the name of a person to ring so that he could make the necessary arrangements on the 'phone. The only question is: 'Why couldn't this have happened in the first place?'

The answer is that someone was following procedures. The best credit card companies, when faced with a situation where their customers haven't paid, contact them by telephone. Why can't banks do the same? If you ask a bank manager this question he will tell you it's because of the time involved (reasonable thinking). However, the procedure described above used much more time that it would have taken to solve the problem on receipt of Roger's first letter.

So often we find customers becoming trapped by their failure to understand an organisation's procedures. It's almost as though they want to make it difficult for customers to spend their money!

It seems a pity to have to identify the Post Office in this example. However, the problem is that while there are now some alternative postal companies, the Post Office is still by far the largest and in most respects operates a monopoly.

If you want to do business with the Post Office, and that means paying them money, you effectively have to have a licence to do so. This is a card that permits you to pay for services by cheque. It is interesting to note that few other business operate in this way.

In our business we often find ourselves issuing large numbers of surveys. On one occasion our card has been returned to the Post Office to be reviewed for a higher cheque limit. An urgent job came in and we needed a very large number of stamps. A member of staff went to

*the Post Office with the cheque book and asked how we
were going to solve this problem. No one knew. The
counter clerk gave us three different telephone numbers
to ring in order for us to solve the problem ourselves!*

*We were passed from one department to another until
we found somebody who suggested that instead of using
the Post Office we could go directly to the franking
department at the central depot, hand over all our mail
in boxes, pay in cash and the mail would be franked. In
order to get some cash we then went to the bank. The
bank teller, on discovering why we needed the cash,
suggested that perhaps we would like to take money in
ten-pence pieces! As things turned out it might have been
a good idea, for when we got to the franking office loaded
with ten pound notes we found that the people who were
taking the letters and franking them were unable to give
any change. Later we learned that if you have a card
which enables you to pay by cheque, you could deposit
unstamped letters at a Post Office. However, there is a
minimum limit. On the last occasion we took surveys to
the Post Office, we found that the limit had increased. We
were sent away! What we had with us would have
complied only with the previous limit.*

If organisations are really thinking 'customer first', they
will recognise automatically that a change in procedures
affecting the customers should be explained to them. At the
very least, they should accommodate their customers'
requirements while the changes are being made.

Don't let changes to procedures make things worse for customers

*An organisation was having problems with credit control (a
euphemism for debt collection). With the help of
consultants they established new procedures for handling
the problem. The customers were to receive a call from a*

> credit control clerk. If the customer agreed to pay, no
> further (internal) action was to be taken. If the customer
> wanted to pursue a query, it would be detailed (on a
> form) and passed to another clerk for batching into 'like'
> problems. Collections of problems would then be passed to
> teams of people whose responsibility it was to solve them.

The new procedure created more work, adding to costs.
More importantly it set the customer on the route of dealing
with more than one person and having two or more telephone
conversations. The impact on customer satisfaction and
loyalty is an unknown cost in situations like this.

When an organisation has problems with credit control
there are two areas that require immediate management
attention:

1. What is causing the failure to pay? (A 'system'
   problem, see Chapter 5).

2. How can we resolve customer concerns in a way that
   creates value or at least minimises customer
   dissatisfaction?

The first will require an analysis of the unpaid accounts
but it should take place in 'our time', not the customers.
Employing quality methods to analyse the problem is the
right thing to do but the purpose is to improve the system's
performance in the future. The customer should remain
unaffected while these analyses are being performed.

The second problem area requires someone to call the
customer immediately in order to understand the nature of the
customer's problem, to *show* the customer that the problem is
understood and to agree a resolution to the problem, or at
least make a commitment to call back and honour it. This
may mean putting the best people into the front line or

getting training organised quickly, but no-one can afford to lose customers.

Meanwhile the problems that create incorrect invoicing should be attacked vigorously with a view to eradicating them. If you set up a bureaucracy, they will be with you forever.

The recent rush of many companies to achieve the quality standard (BS5750 / ISO 9000) has been driven more by market-place demand than a good understanding of quality.

Procedures do not engender enthusiasm

Imagine how the production of quality standards affects the people who do the work. For example, the management announces that all procedures must be written down so that a firm of external assessors can check them. This is not a good way to generate enthusiasm into your workforce! Criticism should not be levelled at the assessors – they only assess against the documentation. Some companies try to document and proceduralise everything, resulting in huge manuals of procedures that no one every needs or uses. The successful companies keep it short, simple and customer-oriented.

There are managers who believe that documenting procedures will solve all the problems of 'fire-fighting'. They dream of a smooth, uninterrupted flow of work. The danger is that rushing to provide solutions can lead to the creation of procedures while the problem is still not really understood.

Putting in procedures is not the way to solve problems

To make this clearer, consider the model in Figure 1. There is work that has to be done as soon as possible (ASAP) and there is work that can be done by a certain time. The four cells describe the sort of behaviour people engage in to deal with the task. Work comes predictably or unpredictably:

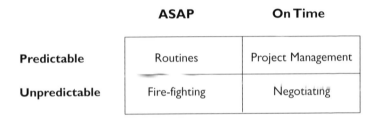

	ASAP	**On Time**
Predictable	Routines	Project Management
Unpredictable	Fire-fighting	Negotiating

Figure 1: Behavioural model of task management

If things are predictable and have to be done immediately, you can establish procedures or routines for them. Like doing the monthly accounts or dealing with common queries.

If things are predictable and have to be done by a certain time, then you need people to 'project manage' them. This means establishing what needs to be done, when it needs to be done by and organising resources accordingly.

If things are unpredictable and have to be done by a certain time, the first thing that happens is that negotiation takes place to establish priority and find the necessary resources. Often the commitment of others must be obtained in order to have sufficient resources to tackle the task.

When work arrives unpredictably and has to be tackled immediately then people have to 'fire-fight'. Fire-fighting consumes enormous resources: managers who hope that new procedures will solve their fire-fighting problems are trying to move from 'fire-fighting' to 'routines' (see Figure 2). This, in most cases, is like putting sticking plaster on an open wound. Usually, it adds to the problem rather than solving it (see 'Quality control at the end of a process is costly', Chapter 5).

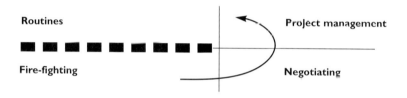

Figure 2: The path from fire-fighting to routines

The model in Figure 2 shows an imaginary wall preventing any direct move from fire-fighting to routines. The only way to solve problems effectively is to take the other route around the model using negotiation and project management skills.

The behavioural logic follows. If you have lots of fires, the first questions to ask are 'type and frequency' questions. 'How often does this happen? Do we have many similar or many different problems? Can they be grouped in any way?'

Having established priorities for action, the manager should map the process flow, which means describing the activities which lead up to the problem in the sequence they occur to begin to establish where the problem originates. He should then try to involve the workforce in finding a solution to the problem: 'Do you know how often this problem occurs? Do you do things here that might be affecting it? Would you like to get involved in helping us solve it?'

With the co-operation of the workforce he can establish process measures that will help everybody understand the nature of the work they do. Once this concept has been grasped, people begin to project manage the problem, monitoring their progress against measures. As the problems get resolved and fire-fighting diminishes, people can then establish routines which they know will work.

Improve first, document second

Looked at this way, procedures become more attractive. Instead of asking for volunteers to document procedures, managers are asking questions, listening, measuring, seeking people's involvement, encouraging people's success and rewarding improvements. If people have enthusiastically solved problems they will be happy to write the solutions down – they will see their value in teaching newcomers. Additionally, they will know that they are allowed to make changes to improve things further.

The secret of success with procedures is improve first, document second. Of course, to do this you have to have a 'culture of improvement' where everybody understands that quality is *the* work, not extra work.

The unreasonable guide – procedures and quality

- Procedures reflect attitude.

- Do procedures make it easy to serve customers?

- Don't let changes to procedures make things worse for customers.

- Procedures do not engender enthusiasm.

- Putting in procedures is not the way to solve problems.

- Improve first, document second.

Chapter 5

Fundamentals of Quality

Understand the capability of your organisation

- Yearly measures of customer satisfaction showed a financial services organisation that 45% of their customers were less than satisfied with the service they received.

- In a telesales organisation it was found that 40% of the calls coming in were from customers with 'post sales' problems (why hasn't it been delivered, it doesn't work, etc).

- A computer services organisation found that 60% of installations were being installed on customer sites behind schedule.

These were all 'system' problems. Within the organisations represented above, the systems are producing the observed results. Information of this nature can provide a useful perspective from which to understand performance. Taking such measures over time often demonstrates that this performance can be consistently achieved as long as nothing changes. Such performance measures reflect the organisation's capability. They may be measures which affect the customer directly (as above) or indirectly.

> Branch administrators in a financial services organisation knew that whenever they sent a doctor's letter covering more than one policy to head office, head office would make the mistake of attaching it to only one policy. It happened consistently.

To view the organisation as a system is the first task for managers who are serious about quality. They need to understand what the system capability is, i.e. what is consistently achieved? To do this managers have to turn away from many of the financial measures (costs, budgets, etc) they are familiar with and look instead at what is happening in the organisation's processes, especially where the organisation has direct contact with the customer.

Some more examples are noted below:

- The 'abandon' rate (customers who gave up waiting for the telephone to be answered) in a teleselling organisation was found to be running at 15-25% every day.

- In a maintenance organisation, certain types of spare were consistently showing 'dead on arrival' rates of 20-30%.

- Again in a maintenance organisation, engineers were consistently achieving between three and four calls per day.

- In a travel company, departures on certain routes were showing consistent lateness.

- An administrative organisation was showing consistent document turnaround times of between two and three days.

Information of this sort tells you what is happening but not why. To understand why, you have to take a look at the work.

Work is a process

Although we design organisations with functional hierarchies, the work that gets done goes across boundaries. Work is a process that goes through functions. Take the simple example shown in Figure 3:

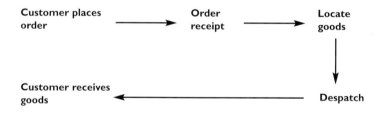

Figure 3: Typical work process

If anything goes wrong in this sequence of events and is not corrected, it is only revealed when the customer receives (or does not receive) the goods or service. By then, it is too late to put things right. This is the problem with quality control; attempts are made to correct things only at the end of a process.

A manufacturer making an annual profit of less than
£200,000 was spending the same amount every year on
engineering adjustments during product installation. As
few as one in six of the products fitted perfectly first time
despite being designed to do so.

Quality control at the end of a process is costly

It is important to know what's wrong at the end of a
process, but action here is costly and largely ineffective
because, amongst other consequences, it increases costs. A
'fix' at this time involves resources that are better utilised
elsewhere; it also decreases the probability of providing a
permanent solution to the problem. People will be inclined to
apportion blame and their prejudices will control their
thinking. Fire-fighting is self-reinforcing in that there are
those who like to have a reputation for solving problems in
this way. Often people have no idea of the importance of a
problem when they set out to solve it (lack of measurement).
Furthermore, the mistakes or waste that have already been
produced will continue if the 'system' is not changed.

An administration organisation 'solved' its backlog problem
by employing a team of people to sort all the mail and
then allocate it to the clerks. Although the backlog fell
and the managers claimed victory, the problem was not
solved. The reason for the backlog was the working
capacity of the clerks. This had not changed. Customers'
mail now waited between receipt and processing but it
was no longer counted as waiting.

A teleselling organisation 'solved' its abandon rate problem
by employing a team of people to pick up all calls and
pass them through to the tellers. It was, at one level, a
good solution; customers were put through to the right
person and no longer passed between tellers.
However, this solution also revealed the number of calls

which were not actually sales calls. The organisation was now in a position to act on reducing non-sales calls (they understood what types they were and how many came in). The same information, however, had been potentially available from the tellers all along. If it had been collected and acted upon, the extra team may have been superfluous.

The costs of quality control are many and include the following:

- Management time spent fire-fighting.

- People's time spent inspecting and checking.

- Exceeding requirements (for example putting extras into deliveries or service just to 'make sure').

- Duplication ('We don't trust them to do it correctly, so we'll check it through/do it again ourselves').

- Lost opportunity (customers who leave you or affect the views of prospective customers by negative word of mouth).

There has been abundant research to show that manufacturing organisations can realise 20-25% of their revenue if they get rid of all such costs. In service organisations, this figure is 30-40% of revenue! What's more, these measures exclude lost opportunity costs, for example the value of customer loyalty and word of mouth advertising.

The problems at the end of a process are usually caused further back (see Figure 4). In fact, problems escalate as they go through the process; what starts out as poor only gets worse unless it is put right at source.

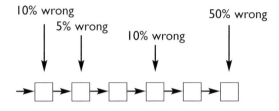

Figure 4: Escalation of problems through a process

> The 10% of 'poor color' problem calls received by the
> telesales organisation were due primarily to inaccurate
> product supply information. The factory saw its job as
> shipping goods according to its production schedule, not
> shipping goods (and information) according to the
> commitment made to customers. Telesellers were making
> commitments which could not be honoured. As a
> consequence many customers called to find out what had
> happened to their goods.
>
> A large proportion of the 'dead on arrival' spares in the
> maintenance organisation were found to be badly
> packaged. The warehousemen were using the same
> packaging for all equipment regardless of its sensitivity.

None of the people involved in these examples was 'at fault'. They were all doing their jobs as directed by their management. In each case the management spent its time dealing with all of the problems that arose in the departments they controlled but failed to work across boundaries to establish the causes.

Managers who work this way essentially ignore work unless it goes wrong. When they do find problems they often jump to solutions rather than working to improve their understanding of the problem.

Improvement comes from attention to process, not function

To put quality to work means two things: Creating 'team' rather than 'departmental' principles through the work processes and developing usable measurement. Everyone doing the work should regard themselves as a member of a team dedicated to the fulfilment of customer requirements and, furthermore, continually able to improve the way they do it.

It is necessary to create a sense of purpose where it is incumbent on everyone to think about their work as a process. This can only begin to happen if people are encouraged to ask the following questions:

- 'What happens at this point in the process that affects our ability to deliver to the customer?'

- 'What do we have problems with?'

- 'How do we know?'

- 'Who else does it well – can we learn anything?'

- 'How often, how much, where, when?'

Ruthless attention to every step in the process will begin to illuminate the problems.

Process measurement is a prerequisite to improvement

There will be no improvement without measurement. You may be familiar with measures of output, but the key to improvement comes from measuring processes (see Chapter 6).

To be in a position to improve things it is necessary to know the extent to which customer requirements are being met. For example, how many orders are being completed within the required times. Output measures identify problems but not the nature or cause. The experience and knowledge of the people who do the work will identify the factors they believe to have an impact on the output.

To understand and act on these factors they must be measured, however imperfectly, lest people fail to learn what creates improvements. People should be encouraged to experiment – there should be some trial and error. In time, they will learn to refine measures down to the ones to help them understand and, therefore, control and improve performance.

Improvement is the goal, not getting performance to standard

It is impossible to know what work a team is capable of producing and therefore fatuous to set targets and standards (see Chapter 6). All that is known is the current production level. Furthermore, any amount of time may be wasted on unnecessary work so true potential is impossible to assess.

Just as there is a 'task' logic to quality improvement, there is a behavioural logic which is complementary. People doing their work with the right methods and measures is not enough, they also need to feel free to express ideas, to problem-solve across boundaries and to take whatever steps are necessary to improve their work. Equally, the logic of quality dictates how managers need to behave. If they stay within the boundaries of their 'function' protecting themselves, controlling their staff's performance and blaming others, nothing will improve.

Operating teams can take responsibility for their own quality

In an ideal situation, there is no reason why an operating team cannot take responsibility for its own quality. Those who do the work are in a good position to improve it if they are given the responsibility to do so. People who serve the customer are the most important group when it comes to service and quality. Consider a typical example of how we treat them:

> *Many financial services administrative organisations have front line staff organised in functional specialities, (for example entering data, checking paperwork, dealing with different functional requirements). Although it is rarely openly espoused, the logic is that if you break work down into manageable functions it becomes easier to control. Staff are taken on, given minimal training and then find themselves dealing with customers – the lifeblood of the organisation. They find they don't have the information or resources to deal with all customer problems so problems beyond their scope have to be escalated to managers.*

An alternative method is to give the front-line staff the means to take responsibility for service and quality. In pioneering service organisations, front-line teams take control of all that is necessary for them to manage the work. This means giving traditional management functions to the staff. Selection, induction, training, performance measurements and quality improvement are all handled by the operating team. One consequence of this approach is that the front line staff are paid more. It represents a shift in assumptions away from pay for status towards pay for contribution.

Managers wary of increasing levels of pay argue that productivity will decline, but organisations which have taken this route find that increases in productivity outstrip the increased costs. The reason is simple; the people who deal with the customer are more capable of getting things right first time. They have the means to continually improve what they do. The other benefit is the experience of the customer when he is dealt with by someone who is wholly capable of meeting his needs. This is of great value to the organisation.

Total Quality Management (TQM) means mobilising everybody

Quality is the creation of value for customers, having customers who are delighted by their experience of the organisation. Total quality is creating value for customers by the most efficient means. TQM entails mobilising everybody in the organisation to improve service and efficiency. To achieve the aims of TQM roles need to be designed such that people are encouraged to behave in a way that allows them to operate on the sources of improvement.

This sometimes means giving front-line teams responsibility for service and efficiency. They should be allowed to take measures of customer satisfaction and given the freedom to take action for improvement. Whether taken on by the team or their first line supervisor, there are two processes or functions which need to be given attention: understanding the customers and understanding the work.

Function 1: Understanding the customers

People do what you count (not necessarily what counts). So if service to the customer counts, the first functional requirement of TQM is to get feedback from the customer in a manner that can be acted upon. (And it doesn't matter whether this function is carried out by the operating team, a supervisor or a manager – it just matters that it happens.) This means that whoever performs this function will be spending time with both the front-line staff and the customer (to get qualitative and quantitative feedback on performance).

FUNCTION I

Operating team   Customer

Purpose: Quality of today's service.

Measurement: Customer satisfaction.

Figure 5: Function 1: Understanding the customers

Function 2: Understanding the work

It may seem silly to say that those who do the work should understand it, but this means more than just knowing what to do when you get to work. If sustainable improvements in service and quality are to be made, people need to understand their work as a system, only when they do so will they have the means for continuous improvement.

Through the appropriate use of measures (see Chapter 6) the team or supervisor needs to understand how performance is affected by conditions within and beyond the team. For example:

1. *In teleselling, plotting the volume of calls throughout the day tells you what levels of resources you need to achieve a good service performance.*

2. *Similarly, plotting the volume of work in and out for many administrative units gives a clearer understanding of capability.*

Differences in the performance of individuals, the quality of procedures and systems, and variation in methods of working are all potential sources of improvement within the team. The first functional consequence of understanding the work is that the team can work on improving its efficiency.

Many quality problems, however, start somewhere else in the process. Understanding the work as what happens in an individual team or function is not enough: it must be understood as a process going from and to the customer. For example:

1. *The ability of service engineers to service customers is governed by the information they have, the availability of spares, the relationship with the customer and often other issues too.*

2. *Demands on front-line staff are increased, often unnecessarily, by incorrect or unclear invoicing, failures in delivery, servicing and so on. All of these matters are within the organisation's control. If the business was being run for the customers, these failures would be eliminated.*

These are systems problems. To solve them attention must be paid to the whole process. This does not mean analysing and reporting problems up and across the hierarchy (a sure way to lose any sense of urgency), instead team members or supervisors should go to all those working in the process and engage them in problem solving and, hence, improvement.

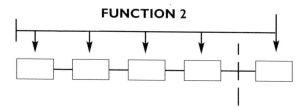

FUNCTION 2

Purpose: Understanding the work to improve performance within the teams and cross the process

Measurement: Efficiency/capability

Figure 6: Function 2: Understanding the work

This is the second functional consequence of understanding the work – knowing what to concentrate on. Whoever is responsible for this needs to be familiar with any operating team's task and must know how well they are currently performing and what may be preventing them from doing a better job (which can only be learned by asking everybody in the process).

Continuous improvement has functional requirements

The two functions outlined above are prerequisites to continuous improvement. Each ensures that measures are in place such that improvements in service and efficiency can be tracked.

In many organisations, a further opportunity exists to find the means for improvement:

Function 3: Comparing performance between units

Where there are many operating units doing the same job, for example where there are a number of branches, their performance measures of service and efficiency/capability should be compared.

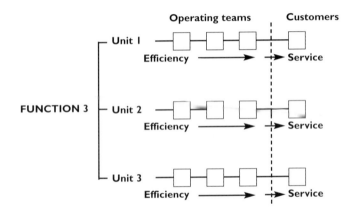

Purpose: Comparative capability

Measurement: Service and efficiency (at unit level)

Figure 7: Function 3: Comparing performance between units

Where consistently different levels of performance are found there is an opportunity to find out why and thus help teams to learn from each other. Differences between units in measures of service and efficiency should alert the manager to ask why this is so. Improvements in performance will be achieved by understanding the causes of variation.

Thinking in terms of the functional requirements for continuous improvement encourages a fresh look at roles, especially management ones. Rather than define the differences between operating team and management roles, it is left to the leader to determine how best the work might be divided in any particular application. What is important, however, is that each of the functions is carried out. Using data concerning customer perceptions, team efficiency and process efficiency is the foundation for continuous improvement.

> *In an engineering services organisation, the engineers took responsibility for customer satisfaction and efficiency measures. Their manager's role was defined by the engineers in terms of the support they needed to serve the customer by the most efficient means. Each of the roles had clear measures against which performance improvement could be tracked.*

When designing organisations from this perspective, we can think less about hierarchy, status and span of 'control' and more about designing roles to add value through acting on sources of improvement. Using information about performance in this way also represents a fundamental shift in people's thinking about measurement. Instead of thinking about measurement in terms of control, it is used as the foundation for continuous improvement. The irony is that moving to this perspective actually improves control of performance as it is now in the hands of those who can do something about it.

The unreasonable guide – fundamentals of quality

- Understand the capability of your organisation.

- Work is a process.

- Quality control at the end of a process is costly.

- Improvement comes from attention to process, not function.

- Process measurement is a prerequisite to improvement.

- Improvement is the goal, not getting performance to standard.

- Operating teams can take responsibility for their own quality.

- Total Quality Management means mobilising everybody.

- Continuous improvement has functional requirements.

Chapter 6

Counting What Counts

The Importance of
Measurement

People do what you count, not necessarily what counts

> *A hi-tech organisation had a repair shop. The
> performance of the people who worked there was
> measured by the volume of completed work. What did
> they do? They repaired the easy things first – anything to
> achieve good measure.*
>
> *The repaired equipment was shipped to branches, where
> management performance was measured by profit. As
> equipment on the shelves represented a cost to them,
> they would scrap all the repaired items they could see no
> need for. The cost of unnecessary repairs was
> extraordinary.*

But the measurement system stopped anybody looking at
it this way. Attention to process would have ensured that only

those items needed for customers were repaired and changes to measurement techniques would have encouraged people not to behave in a wasteful manner.

It is extraordinary that the obvious is so often overlooked in our attempts to understand organisations. Measurement, whether used for reward or not, is the basis for feedback on performance and, as such, will have an impact on behaviour simply because someone, somewhere, is paying attention to it.

The most common sins of measurement are not paying attention to the right things and/or paying attention to the wrong things. Many organisations take measures that actually undermine their capability. To put it more accurately, the measures encourage behaviour that is inefficient and/or not in the customers' best interests.

> *An office electronics organisation counted machine placements at the end of each month. As a result branches offered free trials, put machines out on loan to friends or did anything they could think of to achieve the desired number. The impact of this behaviour on the efficiency of the warehousing/transport organisation was ignored (after all, it wasn't counted!).*

> *An engineering service organisation counted quarterly revenues for its branch operations. This resulted in installation contracts being moved forwards or backwards (to suit branch numbers rather than the customers) and customers being billed for as much 'extra works' as possible in the knowledge that credit notes would have to be issued in the next quarter. Two customers had even paid half the purchase price of their equipment and, after nine months, were still waiting for it to be installed – the problem was that the revenue value to the branch was not sufficiently attractive compared with other contracts in hand. The priority was to meet the revenue targets.*

The intent of measuring revenues at branch level is reasonable – you want to know that the business will perform consistently, i.e. to budget. To use measures as targets, however, will often increase costs and destroy the relationship with customers.

Attention to output can increase costs

A hi-tech organisation measured production in its factories by the volume of goods shipped each quarter. The inevitable result was a rush to ship as much as possible at the end of the quarter. This meant that goods would be despatched to the customers' premises and then left there to await more parts or an installation team. Some sales departments intervened in order to protect their relationship with the customer, but this meant finding extra storage space and double-handling sensitive equipment. Losses were inevitable and the situation was further complicated by other costs because despatch from the factory triggered invoicing so many customers received invoices before they received their goods.

Having obtained an order from a customer and with the assurance of making a profit, it is madness for an organisation to allow its own production targets to create a less profitable situation and alienate its customers.

In a sales organisation the sales order processing department handled a number of bogus orders at the end of each quarter. Salesmen were cheating to make up their numbers. By the time cancellations came through, the work of other departments (manufacturing, buying, distribution, invoicing) was already underway. The quarterly 'hump' created only unnecessary and wasted work.

Using targets can be costly. Some of the costs are obvious, but the most important remain unknown. How much does it cost to deal with complaints, to do things more than once and compile reports on the problems? More importantly, how much does it cost to lose a customer, or prospective customers, through negative word of mouth?

On the other hand, without measures there can be no focus.

> *A financial services organisation declared a mission to serve a selected group of customers with a selected set of products. At the time it was considered to be the critical element in a comprehensive competitive strategy. Five years later it occurred to someone to measure it. Working from data that had been available all along it was found that the mission should have been: 'We'll carry on selling anything to anyone.'*

Without measure there is no focus

In a short time the focus on measurement brought into perspective the real issues faced by management in implementing the mission. The work began five years later than it should have done.

> *Having been through a bad period where they had been selling goods they were unable to service adequately, a sales director insisted to his colleagues that the sales force was now in a position to sell 'only the business we want'. Previously they had been selling 'anything to anyone', a policy which had seriously undermined their capability and created a deeper than usual rift between operations and sales.*
>
> *Despite an extensive communications programme telling them what was expected of them, the salesmen were rewarded on sales revenue (only). The consequence was*

*inevitable: they sold whatever they could to maximise
revenue, and thus, their own remuneration, and it is quite
understandable that they acted in this way. Of course,
everybody in operations was looking for evidence to prove
that the sales director's word could not be trusted. It was
easily found.*

There are two measures of importance for service and
quality: customer satisfaction and efficiency. Customer
satisfaction measures should be taken regularly and used by
the people who deliver service to improve their
performance. To understand how to tackle inefficiency,
managers have to learn to get away from the idea of work
standards.

Measurement for quality demands a move away from standards

However did we get the idea of work standards? There is a
rational notion that people can do so much in a day and this,
therefore, becomes a standard. Managers rightly feel that they
should be concerned with productivity. The extraordinary
thing is that standards become a barrier to productivity
improvement!

Managers want people to produce as much as possible.
To keep control of the work, they count pieces or hours.
The message sent to production workers is, 'Do as much
as you can.' The workforce knows that management is
paying attention to the numbers, so to meet the standard
they do things that are either bad for the customer or
inefficient.

People know that turning out poor quality just to meet
standards is the wrong thing to do. They know what is
wasteful, they know what is detrimental to the customer –

but they feel obliged to meet their manager's demands, if only to save themselves getting into trouble.

Work standards usually include no mention of quality and sometimes it doesn't make any difference how many mistakes are made. More important, not only do standards ignore quality, but they also provide no information about how to improve either customer satisfaction or production efficiency.

If people work to achieve the standard, then the organisation will usually have to endure a certain level of productivity and waste. Sometimes managers keep increasing the standard and people wonder if it will ever end! If you continue to increase a standard you may achieve gains in productivity (essentially through fear) but, most probably, you will also increase inefficiency and customer dissatisfaction.

Why is this so? It is because the new standard is usually set with no understanding of the problems involved in the work process. The standard itself becomes a barrier to eliminating the problems and thus improving the way work is done. If people do achieve the standard, then that is the end of their endeavours. The whole idea is inconsistent with a philosophy of continuous improvement. Employees focus on performance versus the standard rather than the sources of performance improvement.

The costs of bureaucracy associated with recent service guarantee programmes (see Chapter 1), reflect a fundamental flaw in that none of the effort involved will improve the organisation's processes. Committees have deliberated over what might constitute reasonable targets. Bureaucracies set up to deal with complaints will inevitably defend the organisation against many claims. Surely it would have been more cost effective, more honest and certainly more positive simply to be open with the customers about achieved performance, while at the same time making efforts to improve it. What everybody wants to know is whether things have improved. The system, as designed, does not address these problems, being merely an expensive attempt to control waste.

Part of the problem lies in how managers think about numbers. When we think of performance in organisations, we tend to think of how much has been achieved this week or month compared with the last. If people exceed their previous performance we praise them, if performance is down we ask questions or simply tell them to work harder.

The first thing managers need to learn is that managing by single numbers is futile. What you *don't* know from a single number is whether or not the performance achieved is predictable. By plotting numbers over time you begin to ask better questions and thus develop a better understanding.

Measurement should be the means to improve understanding

Compare, for example, two units of an organisation carrying out the same job. Let us call them Unit A and Unit B. If one performs better than the other, the first thing you have to establish is that it really is better. Sometimes numbers, which look different in a 'weekly column', show little actual difference when plotted over time. It is, quite simply, that the numbers vary.

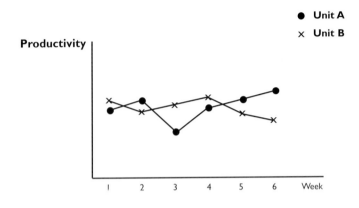

Figure 8: Comparison: productivity per week, units A and B

Typically, managers pay attention to the poor performer when they see the results in week three. All they create is a lot of fuss and bother within the workforce who will do anything they can to achieve the 'standard'.

However, each unit behaves consistently within its control limits, and for the sake of the example it is assumed that the control limits are the same. One can predict that they will continue to perform within their limits provided nothing changes.

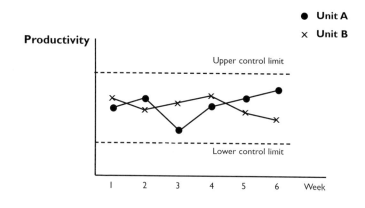

Figure 9: Comparison: productivity per week, units A and B

This is the basis of what is called Statistical Process Control (SPC). Many books have been published that will show you how to plot control charts.

Imposing standards on performance simply encourages people to do whatever they can to meet the standard (and this includes cheating!). Variation in performance provides a limitless opportunity to learn and improve.

Once you have established that the two units *are* performing differently. You can start to ask good questions as to why. In the example given in Figure 10, Unit A clearly performs consistently better than Unit B.

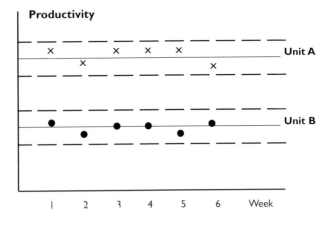

Figure 10: Productivity comparison, A versus B

The difference has to be a difference in method, resources, skill, procedures, attitude, job design or *something*. It can only be found by going and having a look. Of course, the best people to do this are those who actually do the work.

> *A financial services organisation has been managed by attention to daily work standards. Quite apart from the cheating that went on to meet the targets, this method has caused considerable stress to the employees. When the daily outputs were plotted on a chart (see Figure 11) the system was found to be in control. In other words, there was no way that further improvements in performance could be made by simply trying to work harder.*

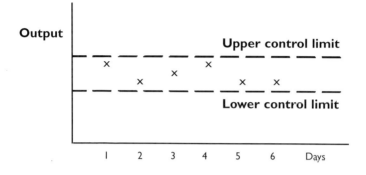

Figure 11: Output control chart

When managers begin to make more intelligent use of numbers, they begin to ask better questions.

> In the course of analysing an administration unit, an adviser plotted two sets of numbers, volume of work in and overtime. (See Figure 12.) What the data showed was that the system was in control. However, managers were authorising overtime just after apparent workload 'peaks' and overtime continued without relation to incoming work.

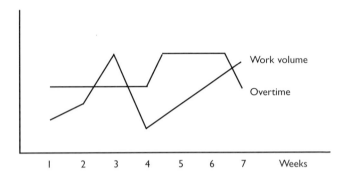

Figure 12: Comparison: work volume versus overtime

The managers learned that not only was the decision to authorise overtime probably wrong but also and more importantly, it continued unnecessarily. In discussion it became apparent that the decision to authorise went up two levels of hierarchy, explaining the delay. The decision to stop overtime was simply a reflex reaction to the cost and bore no relation to the volume of work coming in. These moments of understanding have a profound effect on managers.

When we think of performance in organisations we tend to assume that people will always work at a steady rate. Ideally, this may be the case, but in practice it is often not so.

An administration unit took historic data to plot volume of work in and percentage of work completed. The results were fascinating. (See Figure 13.)

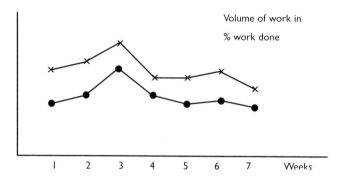

Figure 13: Comparison: work in versus percentage completed

As the workload increased, the percentage completed increased. As the workload decreased, so did the percentage completed! Two hypotheses sprang immediately to mind, namely:

1. There was an accepted 'norm' concerning the size of the backlog.

2. Management behaviour (i.e. making personal contact with the workforce to encourage their efforts) was responsible.

Investigation revealed it was primarily the latter.

What is of interest here is that the example illustrates just how much performance is affected by human factors. The same is true in the following case.

Disturbed by the time being taken to collect customer payments, a finance director employed a team of productivity consultants. The exercise was effective; he saw the average number of days outstanding fall. Some time after the consultants left he became alarmed to see the number rise again. The consultants were called back in and a further improvement was seen. It occurred to someone to plot the numbers and the graph (see Figure 14) confirmed the view that the improvement which had been noted was directly related to the presence of the consultants.

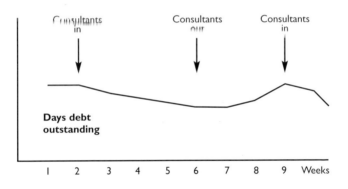

Figure 14: Graph showing effects of consultants' presence on performance

The lesson to be learned from an example like this is that when attention is concentrated on a particular aspect of the work, improvements will be made. However, once that concentration is relaxed the improvement will be lost. This does not mean that it's a good idea to pay for productivity consultants to be on site forever, but it does raise important questions about what is happening in the relationship between the people who do the work and their managers.

Ownership of measures should be with the people who do the work

The key to *continuous improvement* is that measurement should be used by the people who do the work. In all of the examples cited above the statistics were not available to the people doing the work and were used by managers only to compare monthly or weekly outputs.

> A car-hire station, situated in a very busy location, was expected to send meticulous details of daily performance to head office. If the previous day's numbers were not called in by 10.30am, they could expect a call from head office.
>
> The manager had a good performance record. When asked how she did it she produced four graphs. She had been plotting four figures which she considered to be important every day for a number of years. She had found that her charts enabled her to predict rental demand within plus or minus five per cent, thus allowing her to make sensible decisions about how many cars and people she needed. Head office were trying to do the same!

Managers tend to believe they 'own' the numbers. They should not. The numbers should be valued and used as performance measures by the people who do the work. The role of management is to help their staff determine what measures are necessary to find the sources of improvement.

If you find, when you plot the numbers, that a department is in control but shows wide variation, the first task is to reduce the variation. To do this you should ask why the peaks and troughs occur. When a department performs with little variation, improvement can only come from changing methods, or procedures.

A number of companies have reduced the cost of handling supplier invoices by cutting down on administration. They take the view that supplier invoices do not need to be validated. Company policy is simply to pay all invoices on time. Of course, they have limited the number of their suppliers and entered into clear agreements with them, but some people, on hearing of this approach, are inclined to think that the suppliers might cheat by sending in additional invoices. The companies involved, however, are convinced that even if this did happen it would only happen once!

Using measures for improvement starts with thinking differently

Any consideration of measurement as a means of process improvement requires a radical shift of thinking and attitude. Many people attend quality programmes but continue to put a value on output. This can result in extremely wasteful behaviour.

An enthusiastic manager came out of his quality programme full of notions of quality costs and ideas about how time is wasted in organisations. His teacher had opened his mind to the idea of time as cost so he seized the opportunity to measure lateness at meetings. The cost calculations were simple. If a meeting stated 10 minutes late, multiply time by the cost of executive manpower involved and then you know the real cost of wasted time.

This is patent nonsense, which, if pursued to its logical conclusion, will mean reports being compiled to document 'lost time' and the eventual establishment of a 'lost time' reporting bureaucracy. Staff might refuse to deal with customers' problems because they were behind with their 'quality' reports. The fact that these things do happen evidences the folly of not understanding the true value of the 'numbers'.

If you *want* to reduce lateness at meetings set up the following clear social contingencies:

1.   Start on time.

2.   Castigate latecomers (even if it is the MD).

3.   Refuse to reopen matters already decided.

If people experience enough discomfort for coming late they will learn to arrive on time. If the meeting is not of sufficient importance for them to arrive on time then they probably shouldn't be there at all. Whatever you do, don't set up a measurement and reporting system that will only waste time and encourage people to believe they are improving quality when, in fact, they are doing quite the opposite.

The emphasis on output measures reflects the extent to which cost accounting has influenced management thinking. Such thinking is the bedrock of the productivity movement which, because it starts from the wrong place, usually achieves little in terms of quality and often fails to deliver any sustainable productivity improvement.

The unreasonable guide – counting what counts

- People do what you count, not necessarily what counts.

- Attention to output can increase costs.

- Without measures there is no focus.

- Measurement for quality demands a move away from standards.

- Measurement should be the means to improve understanding.

- Ownership of measures should be with the people who do the work.

- Using measures for improvement starts with thinking differently.

Chapter 7

Productivity versus Quality

Attempts at productivity improvement achieve nothing in terms of continuous improvement

No concept has been more misunderstood than that of productivity. For workers a call for increased productivity carries with it the threat of lay-offs. Managers believe productivity to be an economic trade-off between efficiency and product or service quality. The paradox is that when managers focus on productivity, long-term improvements are rarely seen. On the other hand, when managers focus on quality, productivity improves continuously.

Managers were attracted by the idea of improving productivity in a customer service centre. They called in productivity consultants who measured the number of calls received and the number of service people available to take these calls. They then calculated the average time taken to handle a customer query and fed the data into a productivity equation in order to determine an ideal resource level. The managers adjusted staffing levels in line with the consultants' recommendations.

A monitoring system was introduced to 'help' the service personnel. 'Traffic lights' were installed above their work area, with a monitor displaying the amount of time customers were being kept waiting. When the light moved from green to amber it was to signal that customers' calls were being held in a queue. When the light went to red it indicated that customers had been holding for longer than thirty seconds. Productivity declined.

Not only did productivity decline, morale did too. This is a typical illustration. Managers are seduced by the attractiveness of the productivity promise. It seems to stop them thinking about what's actually happening. With systems such as this everything *would* work perfectly if all calls *actually* took the average time, if they came in a consistent flow, required the same amounts of administration and if nobody was ever absent from their station – but life isn't like that.

The staff who dealt with the customers had two complaints. First, the database they used when dealing with customers was unreliable and this sometimes led to calls taking longer than necessary. Second, they estimated that as many as half the calls were from customers chasing progress of an earlier problem. The productivity programme effectively ignored both issues.

A quality approach would have been to tackle both problems by systematically identifying their causes and taking action to reduce them.

> *The monitor showed how many calls were waiting, how long the longest had waited and how many times the red light had been activated in a day. The operators soon learned how to 'bounce' waiting calls so that the system recognised them as new calls. By doing this they could reduce the frequency of red lights, this kept their manager happy.*

In a similar situation, tellesellers learned to accept and then cut off a customer call because this produced better call statistics on the monitor. In these cases morale is so low that people will do anything just to get through the day. They feel that their managers are only paying attention to the number of people at their stations and what's being shown on the monitor.

Information is the means of improvement

Information should never be used to 'control' performance – it should be used to improve it. The same information, used differently, produces performance improvement and high morale in a self-sustaining cycle. Performance information should be used by the people who do the work. In this case the number of calls handled should be reviewed by the people who deal with the customers. They are in the best position to decide what is necessary to improve performance.

> *The number of calls was plotted for five consecutive days. It was found that there were always peaks at lunchtime and at the end of the day. Staffing levels had traditionally never taken account of such fluctuations; the managers insisted that people took their lunch between twelve and two.*

This is not unlike the situation you often find in Post Offices and banks. It's as though the last thing they want to do is have enough staff on duty when the customers arrive in force.

> *By listening to the operators, the managers learned that the system would never improve while they had an unreliable database and customers who found it necessary to progress chase their own calls. The managers worked with their staff to establish the type and frequency of these problems and then undertook to work on solving them in those parts of the organisation where they originated.*

This is an interesting feature of a quality system. The managers are now effectively being measured by their staff. If the managers *are* improving things, the staff will see it – in fact they will be recording the frequency of the problems in order to give feedback on how well things are progressing. People who are involved in improving things are generally more positive and committed than those who are not. And why should their involvement stop here? Why is it that we assume managers are best placed to make decisions about work scheduling and organisation?

Using information at a distance is seductive

Productivity thinking encourages managers away from contact with the real world and towards viewing the business as a spectator. Numbers, ratios and equations become substitutes for reality.

> *A consultant produced his productivity equation for a teleselling organisation. It was as follows:*
>
> $$\text{Productivity} = \frac{\text{Average order size} \times \text{number of orders per day}}{\text{Cost of person per day} \times \text{number of people} \times \% \text{ attendance}}$$

> By following the equation it was argued that productivity
> would improve if an incentive was given for larger orders.
> However, calls were allocated randomly, so if the idea had
> been applied people would have been encouraged to
> dispose of small orders quickly.

It was also suggested that percentage attendance could
be improved by increasing motivation, but the means to
this end was not specified. Indeed, it is hard to imagine
how to motivate people who are treated this way. Pats on
the back and pep talks have little impact if staff feel their
managers are so out of touch with the realities of day-to-
day work.

Cost and quality start from different perspectives

Managers, though, are learning the language of quality
and are attracted to ideas which promote its tenets. Activity-
Based Management (ABM) is one of the latest ideas to be
promoted by consultants. In its message ABM uses the
language of quality process improvement, empowerment and
so on – but in the hands of those with a traditional attitude it
becomes no more than a sophisticated control tool.

ABM encourages the costing of all activities involved in
providing a product or service. In simple terms, the approach
is to map the process flow and then calculate the costs of the
activities which make up the product or service as illustrated
in Figure 15.

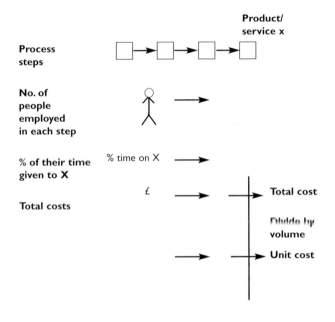

Figure 15: The logic of ABM

Every manager of a unit with an involvement in product or service X is asked to estimate the number of people involved and the percentage of their time given to X. They then calculate the total cost of the work. The information, provided it is reliable, (which is doubtful, but the arguments are beyond the purpose of this book) is very useful for budgeting and pricing purposes, but managers are also encouraged to use it as a means of improving performance. In this regard, the information is not so useful. It might encourage good questions such as 'Why are the costs so high here or there?' – but it is also likely to encourage 'attention to output' and the associated problems of managing by numbers.

Quality demands that you put information in the hands of people who can do something about it

The means of improvement is in the processes. In an administration unit this might mean quality, variability or volume of work in, turnaround times, frequency of errors or waste, and so on. Only process measures will lead to the identification of the sources of improvement, and they can be established and used regardless of the costings associated with ABM. Whether or not such measures are established and used by the people who do the work depends more on their management than anything else.

Managers often become obsessed with their ideas for productivity improvement. They sometimes seem to view people as an unnecessary evil; it would be preferable if people behaved like machines.

> An engineering services organisation introduced a productivity programme. They had modelled the utilisation of engineers, location and availability of spares and distribution of customers. The productivity system would determine everybody's actions; after all, it had worked out how to do things most efficiently. The service engineers became slaves to the system. If they saw wasteful decisions (for example sending spares by taxi instead of exploiting locally know alternatives) they were told not to be negative – they had to trust the system. In a short time, morale and customer satisfaction dipped; the opportunities for improvement were crushed.

To improve service and quality, the people responsible for the work need to be engaged in improving it. Productivity interventions often stifle their involvement. On the other hand, just asking everyone to 'get involved' is just as futile as imploring them to 'work harder'. If people are to be engaged effectively in improvement, managers must provide the focus and the means. These are the prerequisites for empowerment and participation.

The unreasonable guide – productivity versus quality

- Attempts at productivity improvement achieve nothing in terms of continuous improvement.

- Information is the means of improvement.

- Using information at a distance is seductive.

- Cost and quality start from different perspectives.

- Quality demands that you put information in the hands of the people who can do something about it.

Chapter 8

Empowerment

Empowerment should not be confused with levels of authority

> A service organisation launched an empowerment programme. The idea was that if customers had a problem, service agents were free to give vouchers for savings on future purchases by way of an apology. After three months hardly any of the thousands of vouchers printed had been used.
>
> The reason was simple. When you gave out a voucher, you had to fill in a short form and send it to head office. Naturally, nobody wanted to give head office the impression that they were continually making mistakes.

The reason for the form was management's need to be in control. In my experience, when managers attempt to control anything it's a sign that they feel defeated. What underlies management's need for control is the fear that, given their head, the staff might give away the shop. Indeed they might, if they are badly trained, poorly treated and in the front line of a second-rate service.

Empowerment should not be confused with authority levels (i.e. how much you can authorise). When it is, managers become so entangled in making changes to authority levels that they fail to deal with the conditions which would enable staff to use their own best judgement. For managers who are afraid to let staff use their best judgement or who cannot for any other reason increase authority levels, we offer a solution for empowerment which works within existing authority structures.

If a member of staff thinks the right thing to do for a customer involves going above their authority level, they should ring someone who has the authority, explain the circumstances and seek permission. If the decision-maker disagrees he/she must either give an acceptable reason why (for the member of staff has to deal with the customer) or take ownership of the customer at that point.

However, empowerment should not be thought of in terms of how much you can give away. This perspective is too narrow and usually leads to anxiety among managers. Empowerment is concerned with people's freedom, willingness and confidence to act. Sometimes it exists despite management!

> Dave is a supervisor in an engineering maintenance organisation. On his own initiative he had set up a local storeroom for spares that he felt he dare not throw away. Most of his store related to equipment that was 'obsolete' (i.e. no longer sold to customers). After a fair amount of hard work his special store was tidy, organised

*and something of which he was proud because it
enabled him to meet the customers' needs. It soon
became known among engineers that if they had a
problem sourcing a spare, there was a good chance that
Dave would be able to help.*

*One day the regional manager came to visit. He asked
Dave if he could take a look at 'Dave's Den' – he'd heard
about it too! The regional manager instructed Dave to
throw away everything that was not on the current parts
list. Dave explained his reasons for keeping the
equipment, but was told that customers in need of
repairs to old equipment should be visited by a salesman
to sell them up-to-date replacements. Dave's response
was, 'That's all very well, but salesmen are not on 24-hour
call and customers who rent their equipment probably
don't want to buy new.' The regional manager told him
that this was the salesman's problem.*

Dave was not convinced. He kept his store.

No-one knew whether the regional manager had an
important point to make. Clearly he was sufficiently distant
from his people for them not to know, and more importantly,
he was of little value in helping them solve operational
problems.

People have ideas for improvement

Whenever we talk to the people who do the work in
organisations, we find they have ideas for improving what they
do. They know the common customer problems, but can cite
examples of waste and every day they have to cope with things
that don't work well enough. The problem is that their opinion
is not sought and suggestions they may make are not
appreciated. The manager usually has his/her mind on attaining
targets rather than improving anything. I'm sure if we were to

take measures of this situation we would find that the number of ideas for improvement being developed, tested or implemented would be directly related to management behaviour.

Empowerment depends on management behaviour

TQM, or a culture of continuous improvement, essentially means mobilising everybody to improve both service to customers and efficiency, and this can only happen when managers change the way they behave.

> *An insurance clerk had the idea that it would be helpful to have a poster with the names of people in other functions and a brief description of what they did. That way, she thought, she could access the help she needed when dealing with customers. She put the idea into the company suggestion scheme. It was her manager's duty to comment on the idea. He thought that while the idea had merit it might be problematic because people and functions tend to change. He recommended that she receive £25 for the idea but that it should go no further.*

What are the chances that this employee would ever come up with another idea? A better way to respond would have been to tell her to take an hour or two off her normal duties and test her idea with other clerks in the various functions in order to get their views on whether such a chart would be useful and how the idea could be made to work. The manager's job should be to encourage her exploration of the issue and listen to what she learns. If her idea is impractical, she can discover the reasons for this, but most importantly she will feel encouraged to pursue ideas.

> *A shopper was returning a dress to a department store. After the first wash, the colours had run just sufficiently to blur the pattern. At the customer service desk she found*

*herself the victim of an inquisition into how the garment
had been treated. Long pauses ensued while the service
agent surveyed the garment from all possible angles, the
effect being to place more pressure on the hapless
customer who, nevertheless, stood her ground. Finally, the
service agent chose to seek advice from her supervisor.
The supervisor recognised the problem immediately, said
that she had seen a circular on the problem earlier that
week and asked the customer whether she would prefer
a refund or a credit note.*

It was, perhaps, unusually bad for the service agent to be
incapable of helping the customer, but it is extraordinary to
find that she could have been in a better position if her
supervisor had thought about her own job differently.

For empowerment to work, managers have to give up the
idea that they are there to do the thinking while the staff are
there to do the doing. Once managers have grasped that idea,
they then need to realise that empowerment doesn't work by
edict – it requires an enormous amount of hard work from
them.

There are three key ingredients to empowerment: clarity,
participation and support.

Empowerment demands clarity

An empowered person is someone who has a clear
understanding of how their performance contributes to the
success of the organisation. They know that initiative is
valued and that they will be listened to when they have ideas
about making improvements. They think of their managers or
supervisor as supporting their performance rather than
controlling it.

Clarity goes beyond just knowing what the job is – to create the conditions for initiative people must also know what those in other jobs have to do and how these jobs contribute to the success of the organisation. The manager's role is to ensure that staff have a full understanding of the aims of the organisation and are free to get information about both their own performance and that of other departments. Only in these conditions can people confidently take initiatives for the organisation.

Managers in effective service organisations recognise that the people doing the work often have the best ideas about how to improve it. Commitment to improvement increases with effective participation.

Empowerment demands participation

Participation is knowing who to involve, when to involve them and when to make a decision (see Chapter 9).

In good service organisations the manager's role is one of support rather than control. Empowered individuals or work teams meet organisational goals efficiently and effectively and resolve problems with minimal management direction or intervention. The individuals or teams look to the manager for support and are confident in his or her ability to provide it.

Empowerment demands support

The supportive manager is perceived as someone who encourages his or her team to show initiative and take reasonable risks, while helping them to get the best from other units in the organisation. This type of manager provides the information, resources and authority for those who carry out the work. Good performance is rewarded, confidence built and an environment established in which people can work things out for themselves.

> *A service organisation was receiving many complaints from customers. Staff were unhappy too. They recognised that most problems started when customers' complaints were passed from one department to another but not resolved. All sense of urgency was lost and, at the same time, staff were taking calls from unhappy customers demanding to know what was happening.*

> *The solution was bold. The managers locked their offices, got out onto the floor where staff received customer calls and spent their time educating, helping and informing the people who dealt with the customers. Their mission was simple. They wanted an organisation that could meet whatever demand the customer made at the first point of contact. On the occasions when that couldn't be achieved, they wanted to be sure that they could make a commitment to a time to call the customer back and then honour it. The mission became the work. It took three months.*

This is a powerful way to create change. By being on the spot the managers gained valuable knowledge of all the problems their customers experienced and were able to look at their organisation from the customer's point of view. As more problems were solved staff became more confident and competent. Customers were able to contact someone who was capable of handling their needs. Both quality and productivity improved.

Empowerment demands positive expectations

The managers in this case (as with most others) had to give up the view that you can't expect too much from your staff.

> In the course of analysing a professional services organisation, it became clear that the organisation had two distinct halves: the 'boys' and the 'girls'. The 'boys' were the professionals, whose expertise was the source of their revenues. The 'girls' were the typists and administrators who were treated like a necessary encumbrance one had to deal with to get work done. In the midst of the analysis, a girl was found who had grown beyond the accepted norms of responsibility. The girl and the most senior professional in the branch were asked how she had reached her present position.

> The professional recalled that she had decided not to have a family and had sought advice on how to advance her career. She had been advised to sit the general introductory examination for the profession, which she duly did, and this, he asserted, was the reason for her progress.

> By contrast, the girl said that she had sat alongside the professionals and, when she saw the opportunity to take initiative, she had said, 'I can do that for you', and had simply taken the work from them.

That's the key for management. To have an expectation that their staff are capable of taking more responsibility. People in organisations either live up or live down to their managers' expectations of them.

The unreasonable guide - empowerment

- Empowerment should not be confused with levels of authority.

- People have ideas for improvement.

- Empowerment depends on management behaviour.

- Empowerment demands clarity.

- Empowerment demands participation.

- Empowerment demands support.

- Empowerment demands positive expectations.

Chapter 9

Participation

Participation is not just for good times

The board of a hi-tech company had a poor mid-year cash position. The managing director opened a discussion on where savings could be made. True to form the directors looked at each other's areas and were resistant to making cuts in their own. Exasperated, the managing director ordered a 15% cut in costs across all divisions.

The finance director looked after administration and within his province were the biscuits – provided to all who received coffee at meetings. He cut out the biscuits (and other things as well, but they are beyond the point of this story). The negative impact on morale was enormous. It was discovered later that he had considered removing all office plants!

> *The director of customer services, on the other hand, went straight to his front-line workforce, told them of the company situation and set them to work on finding cost savings. Ideas came forward for as much as a 20% saving, but for political purposes he kept his offering to 15%.*
>
> *Customer service division maintained high morale; everyone was contributing to solving the problem. For some time people told biscuit jokes and played biscuit pranks!*

There is a traditional, but mistaken, view that participation is only a 'good times' activity. Innovative organisations accomplish most of their productive changes through participation. Innovative managers – single minded though they are – still get things done by building groups of committed people who feel involved and believe that their contribution is valued.

Participation is the means for getting work done

Participative managers are recognised by their ability to:

1.   Communicate openly.

2.   Establish close relationships with others in the organisation.

3.   Organise frequent team efforts.

These abilities enable them to access the information and resources and gain the support they need to perform effectively.

However, many managers fear participation, they say for example:

'This just means more committee meetings'

A bad situation if this is the case. Some companies do appear to believe that participation means having task forces or committees for everything and they set them up at the drop of a hat regardless of the fact that it might be more sensible to solve some problems in other ways. The task forces often remain in place once they have finished their initial work, or they find more to do and turn themselves into standing committees. Managers, eager to show they are 'participative', count the task forces they have set up rather than focus on what is being accomplished.

'I can't involve my people in everything – it's my job to make the decisions'

This is right – but not quite right. The manager chooses who to involve and when to involve them. There are times when an individual decision is better than a team decision but it is the manager's job to see that the right decisions are made (rather than make them all himself/herself).

Participation is knowing who to involve and when to involve them

The research on leadership and decision-making makes it clear that the use of teams for decision making is most effective for purposes related to staying ahead of change, as follows:

- To gain new ideas and experience.

- To get collaboration, ensuring that many will be trying rather than one.

- To allow those who feel they can make a contribution to get involved.

- To build consensus on a critical issue.

- To allow people who will be affected to influence decisions and hence be committed to them.

- To tackle a problem that goes across boundaries.

- To develop and educate people through their involvement.

There are times when participation is *not* appropriate, namely:

- When one person is clearly the expert.

- When those affected by the decision acknowledge and accept such expertise.

- When someone has to deal with this issue as part of his normal workload (and it would be up to him to form a team if necessary).

- When no real development needs would be met by involving people.

- When there is not sufficient time.

- When people are working well on their own.

- When the decision has already been made.

In the last case, however, it might be of value for managers to invite participation on how best to implement the decision.

Delegation is not abdication. Delegating responsibilities does not mean abdicating your managerial responsibility for monitoring and supporting the work. The manager should stay involved, know what is going on and support the work with information and advice.

'People want to be involved in the big decisions'

This is not true. Initially, at least, most people only want to be involved in local issues, daily annoyances and things they see as inhibiting performance. So many trivial wrongs persistently survive in organisations simply because no-one asked the operators how they might be righted (and even if they had been asked, the operators probably felt that their answers wouldn't be listened to).

> *An agricultural service organisation supplying tractors with drivers allowed the drivers to choose the tractors bought for their use. The owner's logic was simple. Tractor drivers have a habit of liking different machines for different reasons. If he allowed them to choose their own they would be more productive and care more about their machines. He was right.*

It surprises some managers to find that their employees care about and have good ideas about the way their work is organised.

People usually don't feel as informed about bigger issues; indeed they may feel threatened if their contribution is sought. On local issues, people have a lot of experience which they are usually keen to bring to bear on the problem.

'This is democracy gone made'

It could be if you let it, and if you did it would serve you poorly. People do not perform well with unrestricted freedom – you should not let them simply go and do whatever they want. Instead you should help them by establishing the ground rules or limits of the work you want them to do.

Participation requires focus

Without structure, groups flounder. Then everybody concludes that participation is a waste of time.

Despite the best efforts of their teachers, managers often go too far with participation when they begin to make changes. Perhaps this is an over-reaction to the years of dictatorship, more probably it is because the situation is so different. They feel they are on unfamiliar ground and that they can't do *anything* without consulting *everybody*. They have to be reminded that they should not give up leadership. It is the leader's responsibility to provide focus.

> *A director of personnel had engaged consultants to formulate a car policy for a newly created organisation. Through acquisition and merger the current practices were a minefield of inconsistency. The consultants researched the problem and were engaged in meeting to discuss proposals when the managing director burst in. He listened to their proposals and then asked if they had consulted the service personnel who formed 70% of all vehicle users, and for whom the vehicle was a vital part of the job. He was met with blank faces.*

The point is simple. People who spend their time carrying equipment in and out of vehicles probably have important things to say concerning them. This is true with any job – the person who pushes the broom everyday cares about the brooms you buy.

These personnel were not being asked to chose the budget – what's available is available. But showing them that their needs matter and, indeed, are central to the decision, gives a clear signal about what matters – quality of service to customers.

A customer placed an emergency order with a computer manufacturer. Normally these machines would take three weeks to configure and despatch; this customer wanted his in less than seven days. The manager called together members of each department who would be involved and set them the problem. Together they determined a way to do it, got straight to work and delivered the order on time. The sense of achievement was enormous. To be fair, it should also be said that this particular establishment had been working this way for about a year and people considered it normal to be engaged in problem-solving as part of their work.

The unreasonable guide – participation

- Participation is not just for good times.

- Participation is the means for getting work done.

- Participation is knowing who to involve and when to involve them.

- Participation requires focus.

Chapter 10

Understanding Change for Service and Quality

TQM means changing behaviour

All the literature on TQM indicates that a cultural change is necessary if it is to be successful. This is usually where the literature stops. In the pursuit of cultural change, organisations will invest heavily in education programmes, in re-fashioned management development methods and so on. Often, the strategy is one of 'hit and hope'.

Organisations are not helped by those who try to make culture a mysterious phenomenon. It has been described by one commentator as an iceberg, with the various visible parts clear for all to see, but beset by many unresolved conflicts, emotions and other dynamics lurking beneath the surface. This is not a very helpful analogy.

A more straightforward view is to regard culture as, quite simply, the sum of behaviour of the people in the organisation. From this point of view, any analysis and effort for change can focus on people's behaviour.

For example, when an engineer arrives at a house to service a boiler and finds that he does not have a spare, his behaviour will be conditioned by the system in which he works – i.e. the way in which other people (spares, despatch and management) work with him to help him service boilers. To be of use to the organisation, any analysis of this situation must demonstrate a relationship between the way the engineer behaves and the conditions inherent in the system in which he works.

In more general terms, *any* analysis of people's behaviour in organisations must demonstrate a relationship between behaviour and performance. In service organisations embarking on service or quality initiatives we can substitute customer satisfaction and efficiency for performance.

If we accept that quality comes from attention to process, any research must illuminate the processes or conditions governing behaviour, which, in turn, govern customer satisfaction and efficiency.

Behaviour in organisations is conditioned

Figure 16: Model of organisation integrity

The model shown in Figure 16 is built from our research and practice over the last ten years. We assume that an organisation is a system of inter-dependent parts. For any intervention to be successful it must take account of inter-dependency. A change to any one condition is bound to be influenced by, or have influence upon, other conditions.

Sit any manager down to talk about change and he/she will talk strategy, goals, structure, procedures and jobs. Most start with re-arranging the organisation chart. If organisations and, for that matter, humankind were rational this way of understanding and managing change would be sufficient. Human behaviour is driven by attitudes and beliefs. It may be conditioned over time (organisation history) or by other influences (peer pressure, reward systems). Behaviour is also conditioned by structures, procedures, job design and so on.

People's attitudes and behaviour should complement changes to structure and systems, otherwise change will fail. Sometimes change works by happy accident (the people want it and the 'system' will support it) but more often effective change relies on bringing about changes to attitude and behaviour by employing the same systematic approach that we would use to tackle structural or systems changes. In fact, attitude and behaviour change should be driven by the task requirements for improving service and efficiency (see Chapter 5).

Plausible approaches to change fail when organisation conditions don't support them

There have been three general approaches to change in service organisations: customer-first programmes, education for all, and procedures.

Customer-first programmes

'Customer-first programmes' are essentially an attitude/orientation exercise. All too often we discover that people return highly motivated from an excellent training experience only to find an organisation with procedures, systems and other conditions which do not adequately support the values expressed in the programme. People can't delight the customer if their organisation won't let them!

Bank tellers found, following their customer first programme, that they were to use their initiative to satisfy customers **provided** they operated according to the bank's procedures and behaved as directed by their manager. They were not encouraged to question either the procedures or the role of management, even if these were felt to be blocks to good service. The enthusiasm built up by the programme was soon lost, and morale sank to an all time low.

Education for all

Organisations who invest in education for all are usually encouraged to establish a parallel structure headed by a quality steering council. Then follows a series of education programmes and corrective action teams. Following the programmes people go 'back to work' and we find them expressing the attitude that quality is something they do in their corrective action team, or at four o'clock on Tuesdays! Once again, other conditions in the organisation limit the extent of the influence of education for all on people's behaviour.

The board of a computer manufacturer was due to meet as the quality steering committee. In the thirty minutes before the meeting each of them was briefed on their presentations. The scramble to be ready gave a clear indication of the priority that quality held for them.

Procedures

Finally, 'procedures' interventions are often taken on by people who assume that if the procedures are right, quality will follow. Nothing could be further from the truth. There are too many organisations with accredited procedures selling products which don't work very well within a system which has built-in inefficiencies. Such organisations regularly upset their customers.

> *A buyer in a major chemical multinational said that he was looking forward to the day when a supplier would tell him they weren't registered for BS5750 because they considered it insufficient and had developed their own quality system instead. He is not the only person to question the Emperor's new clothes, but he is one of the few prepared to do something about it.*

All such interventions have been undertaken with good intent, and in some organisations they do work very well. However, what we find in many organisations, either by design or accident, is that other conditions fail to support the service and quality initiative.

Any approach to quality or service improvement needs to take account of both sides of the integrity model (see Figure 16). If the left hand side is essentially to do with the systems (structure, procedures, etc) the right hand side is to do with passion (attitudes, principles, etc which govern behaviour). People often describe the difference by using terms like 'hard' vs 'soft', which in itself encourages the wrong perspective, after all how can one be systematic about 'soft' issues.

An associated problem is that while people tackle 'hard' issues with vigour, they accept plausible offerings on 'soft' issues. Knowing that the problem is a 'people' problem, they opt for things with a 'people' label (teamwork, coaching and so on) in the hope that these will provide the solution.

Thinking in this way does not make enough of the interdependence between 'hard' and 'soft' issues. Thinking from a perspective of 'integrity' demands that both sides of the model are seen as interdependent. The task logic of quality (hard) actually demands different thinking and behaviour (soft). We learned in the Seventies that quality circles do not work where they have been introduced without regard to changing the traditional role of the supervisor/foreman.

Today we see organisations with bureaucratic administrative cultures turning quality into a bureaucratic administrative exercise. It is painful, slow and costly. Valuable time is given up to feeding the quality management machine rather than getting on with improving things.

> *Telephone engineers were installing more lines for a small business located in the countryside. They were explaining to the customer that they could do part of the job but they would have to wait for other engineers to complete the rest. Assuming this was to do with unions and 'job property rights', the customer remarked how silly it was. The engineers agreed. They said it was due to procedures laid down by their management. Their own view was that the procedures should provide more flexibility. The customer asked where the manager was. Apparently he had always been difficult to get hold of but now even more so because he was involved in a quality programme!*

Despite the original intentions, quality often becomes a vehicle for sorting out internal problems rather than improving service or efficiency.

> *A manufacturing organisation had established a quality fault-reporting system. While it had been intended that the information would be used to monitor and correct problems, in practice it was used by managers to allocate costs to other departments. Management time was given up to apportioning blame and allocating the costs, enabling them to protect their budgets. Time was not given to solving the problems.*

Change for service and quality begins with a different perspective

A quantum leap in achievement must be predicted on a quantum leap in thinking about organisation design.

The purpose of any service organisation is to create extraordinary value for customers; their delight will be manifest as if they say 'I'm glad I went to ...'.

The customers' experience is governed by the quality of the interaction they have with the front line service personnel. The role of these people, therefore, should be designed to empower them to deliver and continually improve the experience that will evoke such an enthusiastic statement of satisfaction. In turn, the rest of the organisation must be designed in such a way as to support them.

To be successful, organisation design should pay as much, if not more, attention to *how* things will be done as to *what* will be done. High performance organisations rely more on 'loose-tight' conditions to drive behaviour than traditional organisations. This means that clarity of principles and practices (norms) is of greater importance than structure, systems and procedures – the latter being changes as necessary to improve performance.

Three issues should dominate leaders' thoughts about organisation design: principles for high performance, continuous improvement and leadership.

Principles for high performance

The following principles should be considered:

- *Customers:* The measurement and use of customer satisfaction information.

- *Front-line personnel:* The use of self-managed work teams.

- *Management roles:* Designing management roles to ensure attention to process. Adding value rather than levels.

- *Career development:* Development through increasing contribution rather than associating development with hierarchy.

- *Reward systems:* Putting quality first.

- *Systems and procedures:* Designed to support the primary service function.

- *Service over function:* Identification with purpose (service) rather than task (function).

Continuous improvement

The whole organisation should be designed as a self-improving system. Continuous improvement starts with having the right attitude to measurement. Considerations should focus on the identification of key process measures and the provision of measures to teams capable of doing something about them. In other words, we should avoid traditional 'management information' systems and instead develop 'information for improvement' systems.

Process measures should be owned by operating teams and used as the basis for planning and monitoring improvement. Measures and their uses should be considered in parallel with the structural design to ensure that all jobs make a contribution to quality and service.

Leadership

There is no change without leadership. Furthermore, clarity is the single most important influence on performance. For these reasons leaders should be crystal clear about their vision, the principles underlying it, and how they expect it to work in practice. This increases clarity, ensures the principles are understandable and actionable and hence leaders are less likely to be accused of only paying lip service to the vision.

The unreasonable guide – understanding change for service and quality

- TQM means changing behaviour.

- Behaviour in organisations is conditioned.

- Plausible approaches to change fail when organisational conditions don't support them.

- Change for service and quality begins with a different perspective.

Chapter 11

Leadership for Change

Leadership means providing focus

A professional services company whose customers had undertaken quality initiatives was expected by them to do the same. The customers maintained that quality meant turnaround times (for paperwork), whereas the professionals' view was that quality had nothing to do with turnaround times (and strictly speaking they were right) but concerned the technical content of their reports. In industry association meetings the professionals complained to their colleagues about the behaviour of the customers. One or two regional groups even went to the customers to air their concerns, pointing out the customers' failure to deliver documents within specified times. The response to the customers' demands was, 'We'll do the best we can'.

You could argue, in this situation, that the prime concern for quality is to deliver technically correct documentation to the customer on time. After all, service is about making and meeting commitments which satisfy customer needs. If the customers are demanding standard turnaround times, then rightly or wrongly, you have to work out how this can be achieved. If you fail to do this and your failure is evident to the customers, you have no hope of influencing their thinking and every chance of losing them to someone who will respond to their demands.

> *The customers were demanding reports within five days. One branch decided to measure their performance against this standard and found that they achieved it only 60 percent of the time. Many in the organisation took this as evidence that the customer was being unreasonable, although some thought that the branch in question was lacking in achievement.*

In fact this branch was ahead of the others – *at least they knew the status of their current performance!* Only when you know this can you put yourself in a position to improve things.

> *It was easy to obtain information on current performance as the work was logged by administrators. Branches established their current performance, or 'baseline', and then engaged their staff in problem-solving exercises on their methods and procedures in order to establish ways of working which would improve their performance.*

In this way, the organisation moved from a position of having no idea (other than received opinion) about current capability to a full knowledge of the situation, thus they were able to take action for improvement. Once this improvement was achieved, they were able to engage in more persuasive discussions with their customers on working together to improve performance. Much of the work of this organisation depended on the quality of the information provided to them by the customer.

It is the responsibility of leaders to provide the focus. In the above case focus meant establishing measures and ensuring everyone was involved in the improvement process. In general terms, service and quality programmes which set out the desired results with measurable goals achieve success. This does not mean that leaders sit in their offices and declare targets for customer satisfaction, productivity or whatever. First and foremost it means that they get out of their offices to learn more about their currant capability and what affects it.

Leadership means knowing the work

An exercise to get leaders started

While sitting at home, on a train or in your office, take an A4 sheet of paper, divide it into five columns and proceed as follows:

1. In the first column draw a process flow of part of your organisation which touches the customer. In other words, list the activities in the sequence they occur. Draw the process as it goes from and to the customer. If you can't do this you have at least learned a lesson!

2. In the second column put down your ideas of any waste in the process – customer dissatisfaction, inefficiency, duplication, rework, and so on. Now tell yourself *you're* probably wrong.

3. Go to the people in the work process, show them what you're doing and ask for their views. In the third column map the process as they see it and in

the fourth column write down *their* ideas of waste.
Now tell yourself *they're* probably wrong!

4.   In the fifth column put ideas for measurement which
will be useful for understanding how well the
process really works and which may form a basis for
continuous improvement.

This simple exercise puts leaders in a better position to
manage change. Knowing how the system works enables you
to set goals to improve those key areas which have an impact
on service and quality.

> *An organisation found that the biggest problem for their*
> *customers was the speed and accuracy of quotations.*
> *They took too long to arrive and often needed to be*
> *reviewed. When they looked at the quotation process*
> *they found that only 20 percent of the work going*
> *through it was actually for quotations in the sense of*
> *formal tenders. The rest comprised a variety of pre-sales*
> *activities, for example giving the customer comparative*
> *prices, helping the customer decide on a way of*
> *spending remaining budgets etc. These could have been*
> *serviced more efficiently by a more informal method. As*
> *a result of their investigation changes were made to the*
> *work processes and improvement in the quotation*
> *process was tracked by measuring timeliness (time*
> *versus commitment) and accuracy (amount of rework*
> *required).*

Many leaders are not used to getting involved in the
organisation in this way. They perhaps believe that quality is
the responsibility of others. This is indeed true, but clearly the
leaders have a responsibility too. In recognition of this, many
quality consultants, both internal and external, seek ways to
put the fire of quality into the leaders' bellies.

> *An international service organisation recognised that it had to learn to move away from its historic manufacturing attitude ('We sell what we make') to a service attitude ('We'll provide what the customer wants'). Recognising the need to educate the leaders, internal quality experts organised a study tour. The top people were shown excellent companies at work. They were fascinated by what they learned. The conversation remained lively for weeks, but slowly things returned to normal.*

While there are advantages in studying other companies (for example to adopt their ideas or to use their performance as a benchmark), urgency for change is best achieved by taking a look at what is happening where *your* company touches the customer. Similarly, any change should be approached from the point of view of how it will work in this area.

> *Following financial services deregulation, a well-known financial retailer took the opportunity to sell more products through its outlets. The staff in the shops had known many of their customers for years and resented being told to sell more products to them – a message they saw as being inconsistent with providing good service (which was a core value espoused by their board – see below). They were being asked to change from 'nice tellers' to 'active sellers'.*

To be successful some financial retailers *will* need to sell more products to their customers and enlarge their customer base. These are relevant strategic concerns. But the strategy will only be successfully achieved if the leaders consider how best to achieve it from their current position. Otherwise, they run the risk of being vulnerable where they least want to be – in front of the customer.

Leadership means mobilising everybody

Having focused on what they want to achieve and how
they want to achieve it, leaders must take responsibility for
mobilising their staff. If they want to provide excellent
service, then every opportunity must be taken to tell them so.
Equally, they should make time to listen to people in order to
find out what they need to enable them to give exemplary
service. Everything that gets in the way of service and quality
will be in the system somewhere – it's the leaders' job to find
it and pay attention to it. If the leaders pay attention to these
things, everybody else will too. In organisations where
'quality education for all' has had success, the results are
largely attributable to the leaders' behaviour.

> *A manufacturing company sent all of its managers on a
> quality education programme. On return, the graduates
> found themselves being sought out by the managing
> director. He wanted to know what they had learned, how
> it could be applied to their organisation, what plans they
> had, what measures they thought were important, when
> they were going to start and how soon they expected
> results. He told them he'd be back to find out how they
> were doing.*

With leadership like this you might wonder if the
education was necessary! The leader was providing the
passion to inspire others. Leaders can provide the framework
for action ('If you have any doubt, decide in favour of the
customer' or 'Use your own best judgement'). If they are
familiar with what goes on in work processes, leaders can use
such principles to guide people's thinking thus giving them
the scope to decide how best to act in any particular situation.
The recognition that 'principles' or 'values' are the key to
high performance has lead many organisations to promulgate
'values statements'.

The board of the financial services company referred to earlier worked for some time to create their 'values statement'. They settled on four primary values, each exemplified by a single word, and commissioned consultants to develop a communications programme to cascade them. A handbook was developed with definitions of each of the values, examples of working practices and an assessment device for teams to use.

At first glance it would appear that a good job had been done. However, when the communications programme got to the cascade of the third value statement, voices in the organisation loudly proclaimed that the executive group should stop. The complaint was that they were not living up to the values they claimed to espouse. Active selling was seen to be inconsistent with customer service.

On inspection of the handbook it was clear to see why the charge had been brought. The definitions of the single word value statements were little more than an ill-defined pot-pourri of attitudes, values and ideas. Practices which were supposed to exemplify the values covered such a range of ideas that people easily become confused when working through the document.

By the time they had reached their 'action', it was possible for people to be way off the 'target' as others perceived it. Hence, what was evidence of the value in action to one person was irrelevant or even counter-productive to another.

Leadership means providing clarity

To be effective, values or principles must be capable of being translated into action. It is the leaders' responsibility to think the problem through and to do this well they must test any principle against concrete knowledge of what goes on in the organisation. When communicating values or principles, leaders need to give specific illustrations of what they would expect to see in different circumstances. They also need to recognise that some people will struggle with making sense of the action they are expected to take and should seek such people out for discussion.

> *A customer was impressed by his holiday tour company. On arrival at his resort he found all of his needs catered for in an unobtrusive way. It was as though the local representatives already knew what he'd need to know and what arrangements he'd want to make.*
>
> *During one of his many early contacts with the representative he asked, 'How did you decide to do all this?' The representative was surprised to be asked. 'Well, it's the way we treat everybody,' he replied. 'We've listened to what our customers say they need when they arrive and we've worked out ways to make it easy for them to get on with enjoying themselves.'*

The leaders had worked hard to translate a service mission into practicalities – in this case many simple everyday things. In most cases, the leader will need to pay attention to whole 'processes' in organisations to see how matters of structure, systems, procedures, attitudes and so on are helping or hindering the changes they seek.

> *It was February. A customer asked for a child's winter vest in a high street retailer which had a reputation for good service. She was told that the winter range was no longer on sale. She asked the assistant to check the stockrooms, which was done, but to no avail. The assistant sympathised with the customer and explained how she solved the problem for her children by buying ahead. They agreed this could be costly as children grow in spurts and are fickle about wearing clothes which do not fit well.*
>
> *It occurred to the assistant to mention that among the many mothers who had experienced this problem was a woman who had previously been a buyer for the*

organisation. Apparently she had commented that the experience had shown her how foolish it had been for the buyers to use national demographic information and purchasing patterns to decide what would sell (as she had done) instead of asking what mothers wanted to buy.

The assistant also mentioned that the company had been criticised by a television programme for failing to stock what the customers wanted (when they wanted it). This had resulted in a new procedure. Each branch now completed a weekly form for head office on which it documented customer requests and comments.

The customer asked if the form had led to any changes. The answer was no.

You can imagine what's happened here. In response to consumer criticism a procedure has been established. Unfortunately the information goes up a hierarchy instead of where it might be useful (in buying). It is probably being collated, questioned and compared. Certainly it isn't being actioned.

Leadership means taking responsibility for the whole system

It *may be* that no action is the right response. But if that *is* the case the people working in the shops should know why no action is being taken, otherwise they will think that no one really cares about their reports. They will feel less encouraged to listen to customers and will be less able to deal with customers who have problems. The managers don't see all this as a process. Whoever felt sufficiently concerned to order the collection of information did not have an equal passion to ensure it was used – the system was allowed to stifle it.

Dependent on hierarchy, failure to attend to process, the misuse of measures, poor attitudes and lack of freedom to take initiative are all strong candidates as conditions contributing to this apparent failure.

> *The leaders of a service organisation had successfully introduced a new customer survey. They were using their own staff to do it. The staff had interviewed a number of customers and then surveyed many more by means of a questionnaire. The results were impressive. Interested in extending the use of this survey throughout its operations the international management team asked for a review. They learned that the survey was not, by itself, the answer. Results were achieved because the workers used the data to improve performance (empowerment); the managers and staff solved the problems that created customer dissatisfaction (attention to process) and, above all, the leaders were totally committed to finding ways to make it all work.*

It's the whole system that puts the tool to use and the leaders' job to think about it in this way. There is no change without leadership. Leadership towards quality and service improvement will be largely ineffective if it is not based on a wholly different way of thinking.

The unreasonable guide – leadership for change

- Leadership means providing focus.

- Leadership means knowing the work.

- Leadership means mobilising everybody.

- Leadership means providing clarity.

- Leadership means taking responsibility for the whole system.

A message to managers

If you have finished reading this book and found some valuable lessons in it, then this is not an ending but a beginning. The quest for service and quality is one which pervades every aspect of an organisation and the starting point is a comprehensive understanding of the work processes, the workers and the customers.

Creating an environment where staff feel free to voice their opinions and use their initiative is a useful step in fully involving them in any problem-solving process. Customers too should be consulted on matters of service and quality if they are to perceive that they are indeed of value to your organisation – where would you be without them? However, customers and staff cannot effect improvements to service and quality on their own. The initiative must come from management, and if they are to succeed in this endeavour they must first cast aside traditional thinking about their role and take responsibility as motivators and leaders of a team all working to the same goal.

It is not difficult to incorporate these ideas into your strategy.

> *Early on in their quality programme, a financial services organisation decided to find out what their customers thought of them. They conducted a number of interviews with their customers which led to a decision to survey many more on the issues which seemed to matter most to those they had already spoken with. In this way they could obtain quantitative information which, by its nature, would be much more useful in driving change.*
>
> *It was decided to conduct the survey by telephone interview. Discussions ensued about how many people to train as interviewers (they had already decided, quite rightly, not to use an external agency). Then someone had*

a brilliant idea:'Let's use everybody!' On the days chosen for the exercise, staff finished work at the normal time and went voluntarily to a briefing.They then 'phoned as many customers as they wished and recorded the results on the survey form.

A barbeque was held in the corporate garden afterwards to allow the volunteers to socialise and exchange ideas. The impact of this plan was extraordinary and quite beyond everybody's expectations.

People at all levels in the hierarchy were talking about what they had learned; some customers needed immediate help, almost all were delighted to be contacted by someone from the company and very few were uncooperative.

The energy and enthusiasm was infectious and everybody, from chief executive to postroom clerk, was involved. What began as an exercise in gathering data from customers turned into a cultural transformation. Everybody's attention was focussed on customers – hierarchy and status become irrelevant. Managers, by their own admission, were surprised at how well and enthusiastically their people took to the task.

The whole event overturned the opinions of the cynics who had believed the customers would not want to be involved and that the staff could not be expected to perform the task in a professional manner.

The ideas expressed in this book are capable of providing a powerful catalyst for improvements in service and quality, but you – the managers – are the agents for change and it is in your power to achieve extraordinary results. You never know what can be achieved until you try, and you may even surprise yourself!

Further information

If you would like details of any other Vanguard Education publications, or would like to know more about Vanguard Consulting, then please contact the address below.

Vanguard Education Ltd
Villiers House
1 Nelson Street
Buckingham MK18 1BU

Tel: 01280 822255
Fax: 01280 822266
www.lean-service.com

About the author

John Seddon trained as an occupational psychologist in Wales and then London. He has spoken and lectured at a variety of conferences, universities and schools of management and has a reputation for being controversial but informed.

John's early career was concerned with changing behaviour in organisations. When his work began to take him overseas he developed an interest in the impact of ëcountry culture' on organisation behaviour. This, in turn, led him to question much of what was accepted tradition in management education and training.

John is managing director of Vanguard Consulting Ltd, a consultancy specialising in organisation change.

The first Vanguard organisation was established in 1985. Vanguard set out to approach changing behaviour in organisations in a more systematic way than it had been treated to date, rejecting plausible theories for practical empiricism. Vanguard quickly developed a reputation for effectiveness.

When asked to audit quality programmes to determine what had limited their success. John found good ideas being implemented with little understanding of how to address the problems of changing people's behaviour. Since those early experiences, Vanguard has been pioneering new methods for the effective introduction of change for performance improvement.

Also by the author

"The Case Against ISO 9000"

Oak Tree Press, 1996, revised 2000

John Seddon and the Vanguard team
have also written a CD-ROM and a series of
guides and manuals.

These are listed on the Vanguard website:
www.lean-service.com